CLOSE AIR SUPPORT

CLOSE
AIR
SUPPORT

An Illustrated History, 1914 to the Present

Peter C. Smith

ORION BOOKS/NEW YORK

To Dr. Ira Chart—with sincere thanks
and gratitude for all the generous help, kindness,
and support down the years.

Published by Orion Books,
a division of Crown Publishers, Inc., 201 East 50th Street,
New York, New York 10022. Member of the Crown Publishing Group.

ORION and colophon are trademarks of Crown Publishers, Inc.

Manufactured in the United States of America

Library of Congress Cataloging-in-Publication Data
Smith, Peter Charles, 1940–
    Close air support : an illustrated history, 1914 to the present /
by Peter C. Smith.
        p.   cm.
    1. Close air support—History.   I. Title.
    UG700.S538 1990
    358.4′142—dc20   89-36702
                                                                  CIP

ISBN 0-517-56907-8

Book Design by Shari deMiskey

10   9   8   7   6   5   4   3   2   1
First Edition

Contents

Author's Note

The term "close air support" can be used to include all air attacks that are coordinated with the supported ground forces. High-altitude bombing of enemy positions by heavy, level bombers in advance of friendly forces, or helicopter gunship support of troops in the field, in this context, can quite fairly be called close air support. But for the purpose of this study, the above-mentioned categories are not generally included. Although the delivery method is technically not a criterion, close air support in this volume refers in the main to those missions in which fixed-wing pilots, under the direction of an airborne or ground controller, visually acquire or are radar-directed down to low-level targets in the close proximity of friendly ground forces.

Close Air Support: An Overview

Almost as soon as man invented a wondrous machine that enabled him to take to the sky its potential as an instrument of war was being studied. Indeed, visionary writers of fiction such as H. G. Wells, Jules Verne, and a thousand imitators had long prophesied the coming of aerial warfare and had uttered dire predictions of the havoc that would result.

Initially the frail wires-and-struts aircraft of the early 1900s were barely capable of carrying their human pilots, let alone the additional weight of armaments. Development was rapid once initiated and, within a few scant years of Kitty Hawk, flying machines had become quite capable of adaptation for warfare.

Cooperation with army and navy activities was the natural role assigned to these early military aviators. To the military mind of the day the airplane seemed merely a useful appendage to these traditional services. The chief merit of aircraft in both cases was to extend the range of reconnaissance and thereby give the advantages of early warning and the plotting of troop and naval movements. Even though scouting was the logical role of aircraft in the warfare of 1911 onward, it was but a short step from that to "armed reconnaissance." Under this gradually developed system, aircraft equipped with primitive forms of explosives could now not only locate and report the enemy spearheads but attack "targets of opportunity" where these presented themselves. Once this principle had been established, the creation of more and more specialized aircraft to conduct these "bombing" missions followed. The creation of the bomber aircraft as a distinct type of flying vehicle was hastened along its gestation period by the cruel and demanding forcing ground of World War I after 1914.

Thereafter, from being merely a useful "third arm," the bomber made enormous strides in both its carrying capacity and its range. By 1918, both Great Britain and Germany had squadrons of long-range aircraft quite capable of delivering lethal cargoes of death to the other's capital cities. The slippery path, which led inevitably from experimental novelty to terror weapon, took but a decade, such is man's warped ingenuity.

The creation of a wide variety of bomb-carrying airplanes led many nations, such as Great Britain, France, and Italy, to set up distinctive air services quite independent of the two older arms. Even where the air forces remained nominally part of the navy and army, as in the United States and Japan, their air-minded leaders developed their own distinct and vociferously independent strategy. Between the wars these strategies crystallized into two main schools of thought, the Strategical and the Tactical. The former, with high-profile proponents like General "Billy" Mitchell in America, Lord Trenchard in England, and General Giulio Douhet in Italy, claimed that the long-range heavy bomber, directed against civilian targets, would win wars unaided and unassisted by armies or navies. Such a policy was simple and alluring in the new "air age." To nations weary of the slaughter on the western front it seemed to offer a cut-price means of waging war by fear.

In fact this policy was to prove a costly chimera in terms of both lives and money. The blitz of London and the firestorms of Hamburg and Tokyo produced a steely resolution in civilian populations rather than cowing them. Four years of intensive day and night bombing of Nazi Germany by vast fleets of four-engine bombers *increased* its war production rather than defeating it, published figures clearly show. Armies and navies were proven to be as essential as ever. Neither armies nor air forces could operate at all without the supplies brought in under the protection of the navies. Nor could they take the war to the enemy without being landed by navy or given the land to operate from by an advancing army. Other than Denmark, no nation ever submitted without enemy soldiers setting foot on its soil, until the advent of the atom bomb.

If armies were necessary, then those armies that had most adapted the air weapon to its cause at the front line were the ones that triumphed. So the Tactical school of thought finally had its day in Britain and America; it had never lost its place in Germany and the Soviet Union. Thus World War II ended with the triumph of close-support aircraft.

The very atomic weapons that finally made Strategical air power a viable concept again in 1945 had, by their all-consuming nature, made it impotent. A standoff situation developed which led finally into the era of MAD (Mutually Assured Destruction). When the two military camps of the postwar world found themselves in the straitjacket of their own nuclear power, then the Tactical application of air strength became the only means left for them to use the power of the air-delivered weapon in war. The lesser powers had never stopped using air support tactically.

Nor did the advent of jet aircraft alter this concept. One lesson that had been paramount during World War II was that if close air support was to be effective, it had to be closely coordinated, flexible, sustained, and accurate. Initially jet aircraft were not as accurate as their forerunners, nor could they "linger" over the battlefield. Eventually the Korean War, the various Israeli/Arab conflicts, and the Vietnam War all refined techniques still further and demonstrated the power of close air support by jets.

With the postwar development of the offense came, as always, new weapons of defense: antiaircraft missiles, hand-held and guided to their targets with increasing sophistication. These forced the close-support aircraft farther from its target and triggered yet more counterweapons, the "standoff" bomb of the heat-seeking, laser-guided variety. The introduction of the helicopter as a potent and valuable army support weapon has led once more to the wheel coming full circle.

It is the study of the ultimate expressions of fixed-wing tactical air power, as they were developed, used, and countered, that concerns this history. We will examine just what the term "close air support" meant to different combatants at different periods and in different conditions through the eight decades that aircraft have been an essential ingredient of any general's battle plans. To illustrate this "state of the art" down the decades I have selected eight main areas of application: (1) initial combat during World War I; (2) small-scale colonial and internal conflicts between the wars; (3) further trials and experiments in the larger international conflicts of the 1930s; (4) varying applications and techniques by the combatants in World War II; (5) applications in the postwar colonial disengagements wars; (6) reappearance of close air support in the Korean War; (7) refinement during the Vietnam War and Arab/Israeli conflicts in the 1960s; and (8) current theory and hardware.

Forging and Applying the Weapon

The invention of the flying machine was almost immediately followed by its military use. The very first aviators took their products to the military authorities to demonstrate their potential. Orville Wright, for example, demonstrated his machine in Washington, DC, in September 1908. He reported back to his brother Wilbur that army personnel there "think the machine is going to be of great importance in warfare." How right they were, although US Army Lieutenant Thomas Selfridge, making a military test flight, paid for his enthusiasm with his life in a subsequent crash. The army did not actually purchase its first Wright Flyer until 1909. In October 1911, Lieutenant Riley Scott demonstrated the accuracy of air attack by dropping bombs on a target at an exhibition on Long Island. Nobody in America showed much interest and indeed, despite its initial lead, US military aviation fell steadily behind developments in Europe.

Early applications of aircraft for carrying and delivering high-explosive ordnance in support of armies in the field predated World War I. One example was afforded by the American aviator Leonard W. Bonney who flew scouting missions in the Mexican revolutionary war of 1913 in a Moisant aircraft. Mexican army engineers designed a "spherical dynamite bomb" exploded by means of a rifle cartridge. He dropped these bombs on suitable enemy targets at the end of a dive. Bonney had already absorbed one basic tenet of flying close air support. Rifle fire from the ground damaged his machine and exposed its vulnerability.

This was basic bombing by eye, of course, but there was no lack of inventive endeavor in applying the current technology to improving the capabilities of aircraft in this respect. On 9 July 1913 for example, M. Henri Coanda, a Paris engineer, submitted a specification in an application to the London Patent Office for a "projectile discharging tube" for "the armament of aircraft and the formation of fighting units." His ingenious device consisted of a charging device in which projectiles were stored on board the airplane in order to be successively introduced into a discharge tube. The operator worked the lever "causing the expulsion of the projectile from the tube, the introduction of a fresh one into the tube and the compression of the spring actuating the expulsion piston."

From such basic ideas and applications was the bomber born. The French army began purchasing aircraft and training pilots in 1910 and a year later created an Inspectorate of Aeronautical Services under General Jacques Roques. The Germans followed with their Inspector of Aviation Troops, but at this point both these nations were thinking more in terms of reconnaissance than active participation for their machines. During the Italian seizure of Libya from Turkey in 1911, their invasion forces were initially pinned down in their coastal bridgeheads. Scouting flights were made into the interior to access the opposition and on some of these missions Italian planes dropped a few small bombs on Turkish columns.

By 1912 the British army specifications for an aircraft for military purposes included a 350-pound payload. The outbreak of war between the major powers in Europe in August 1914 heralded four years of unprecedented expansion in aerial warfare. With the carnage and deadlock of trench warfare on the ground, any means of carrying the fight to the enemy from the air was utilized with vigor.

The use of scouting airplanes was given official status by the British army in the field as early as October 1914. The Royal Flying Corps (RFC) instructed Major Maurice Musgrave, the army officer in charge of British army airplanes in France, that "Several instances have occurred lately in which targets suitable for attack have been passed over without any action being taken. In future all aeroplanes carrying out reconnaissances will carry bombs and whenever suitable targets present themselves they should be attacked by dropping bombs."[1] The need for precision was soon stressed, which led to calls for these attacks to be pressed home despite the hazards of return fire. In February another directive to RFC pilots stressed that accuracy to within 50 yards was essential. If it could not be obtained from heights of 5,000 to 6,000 feet, the target had to be attacked at low level—500 feet.

In the Far East, Japan, main ally of Great Britain, contributed air-

The Royal Flying Corps was an early and enthusiastic embracer of the close support weapon. One of the most outstanding victories attributable to ground-attack aircraft took place against the Turkish army in Mesopotamia during World War I. Here a BE2c of No. 30 squadron, built by the Royal Aircraft Factory, is fully bombed up on its desert airstrip, ready for an army support mission in 1916. (RAF Museum, Hendon, London)

craft equipped with bombs during the final days of the siege of the German treaty port of Tsingtau, China.

By 1916 both British and German aviators were flying low-level missions in support of advancing troops as they struggled across European battlefields. England's Lord Trenchard's dogged policy of continual patrols resulted in proportionally as bloody a cost in the air as the British army was suffering on the ground. More than five hundred British aviators became casualties during the Somme battle, more than 100 percent of their original number. Even at this early stage the British were reluctant to admit that this form of warfare called for its own types of aircraft and techniques. As in all later conflicts they spurned such expertise and instead wholeheartedly committed all their fighter aircraft to the fray as a matter of course, with neither rest nor relief. Men flew several low-altitude missions a day until they were eventually shot down and killed or wounded.

At the Battle of Cambrai all types of aircraft were used. Under the command of Captain R. H. Jerman, the 3d Brigade of the Royal Flying Corps had been built up to a strength of fourteen squadrons, with the

The very young Lieutenant Gunter Schwarzkopff (second from right) poses with another officer and his ground crew at an airfield on the western front in 1918. Schwarzkopff flew ground-attack missions flying with the German army. Schwarzkopff later transferred to the Luftwaffe and was instrumental in the early formative years of Stuka training and techniques. He became known as the "Stuka Father" and upon the outbreak of World War II led the famed St.G 77 ("The Luftwaffe's Fire Brigade") in its missions against Poland, Belgium, and France, before being shot down over the Meuse. (Peter Schwarzkopff)

The introduction of the tank by the British on the western front in 1916 and its further use in 1917 and 1918 caused the Germans much consternation. Attacks by low-flying aircraft to "strafe" these lumbering monsters proved one very effective way of restoring the balance.

This photograph is an aerial view of a French town taken by German fliers after a successful strafing attack had held up the British advance. Knocked-out British tanks can be seen in the center of the photo on the main street. (Bundesarchiv-Militararchiv, Freiburg) new Sopwith Camel fighter supplementing the established Bristol Fighters and de Havilland types. In all there were some 275 aircraft on hand and a large proportion of these was allotted the task of supporting the first wave of the British infantry attack by machine-gunning the enemy trenches to keep their heads down while No. 35 Squadron was to assist the Cavalry Corps by scouting and bombing ahead of them in the event of a breakthrough.

Strafing was done at ground level with Vickers or Lewis machine guns on enemy troop concentrations. The British fighters could also carry up to six of the little 20-pound "Cooper" bombs under their wings to be dropped on targets of opportunity. Ground level meant what it said as witness the oft-quoted report by a German officer that he had been knocked flat by the wheels of a British SE5a. The Royal Flying Corps was effective but that efficiency cost greatly in machines and men. RFC ground-attack squadrons took up to 30 percent casualties during these operations, a horrifying figure which later did much to turn the Royal Air Force (RAF) against the concept of close support. The number of aircraft per squadron was increased from eighteen to twenty-four during the last year of the war and they helped stem the last great German offensive in March 1918.

Just how traumatic their ground-attack squadrons' loss rate had been was made clear by Wing Commander J. C. Slessor, who, in a series of lectures delivered as late as 1936, clearly pointed out just why the RAF (as the Royal Flying Corps and Royal Naval Air Service had become in 1918) was no longer interested in close air support. The 30 percent casualty rate taken at Cambrai was matched during the RAF's commitment to halt the German offensive in the spring of 1918. He gave as an example the experiences of No. 80 Squadron RAF, which was almost constantly engaged in army-support missions from March until the armistice in November. The average strength of the squadron had been 22 officers but during that ten-month period they had lost 168. This gave a squadron loss rate of 75 percent per month.

The other combatants were less prodigal with their manpower and more attuned to the need for expertise. The French answer was the formation of their Division Aerienne strictly for ground-support missions. Instead of using any nearby fighters for the job like the British, their allies moved this large group around at the front to where it was most needed. In this method of application the French somewhat anticipated the concentration of force concept utilized by the Luftwaffe in World War II, especially that of Fliegerkorps VIII.

On their part, the Germans quickly adopted similar measures, and at Verdun in 1916, their fighters were employed in ground-attack work.

General Oskar von Hutier incorporated this in his World War I concept of mobility by which enemy land strongpoints would be bypassed by the ground troops and left to be mopped up later rather than attacked head on. Thus the German advance would not be slowed down.

All this emphasis on speed and flexibility resulted in two innovations that other powers eventually imitated after the Germans had perfected them. The use of specialized formations especially trained and skilled in aerial ground-strafing, the Schlachtstaffeln, was the first. Initially each of these units was equipped with six Halberstadt or six Hannoverana aircraft, whose pilots were trained to attack from an altitude of 200 feet.

The second significant German idea was the construction of aircraft fitted with armor protection for the pilot and the vulnerable parts of the engine. These were the Junkers JI and Junkers CLI. They supplemented their normal strafing machine-gun attacks with bundles of grenades against concentrations of infantry. Again the British were forced to copy this idea, but their equivalent machine, the Sopwith Salamander, arrived too late to take part in the war.

The introduction of the tank to land warfare gave new scope for aircraft, both as a partner and as a defense. Working in conjunction with the tanks, low-flying aircraft could open up gaps in enemy lines and exploit them. But the Germans saw the aircraft as a quick and flexible method of countering Allied tank thrusts by low-level machine-gun fire and bombing. It was by this method that they were able to reverse the British tank victory at Cambrai in November 1917 by a counterattack on 30 November. Here one British observer, Captain Geoffrey Dugdale, noted: "The German aeroplanes were very active, flying over our lines in large numbers, very low. They were shooting with machine guns at the troops on the ground, and I am quite sure this did more to demoralise our men than anything else."[2]

On the very first day of the German counterattack the British 35th Brigade HQ was cut off. A breakout attempt was led by Brigadier General B. Vincent but this was broken up with heavy casualties as a direct result of intervention by hordes of low-flying German aircraft. The few British survivors had to seek refuge in Gauche Wood. At Banteux ravine the German strafers cooperated with the German Caudry Group to overrun artillery positions as they forced the British infantry retreat.

Thus were born the outlines of the blitzkrieg and the tank-busting roles of the airplane, both basic ingredients of close support ever since. A major factor noticed by Dugdale was the effect on the morale of seasoned front-line troops by the very appearance overhead of unopposed enemy aircraft. The troops were reluctant to mount attacks in the open when German airplanes were about, which restricted the speed of British operations.

The first successful antitank missions were flown in March 1918. The pilots involved were Oberleutnant Robert Ritter von Greim, who was the Staffelfuhrer of the 34 (Bavarian) Jagdstaffel, and his wingman, Vizefeldwebel Putz. In missions conducted in the area of the old Somme battlefield they attacked a column of advancing British tanks. Their method was to dive down from an altitude of 600 meters and strafe them with their machine guns. The tanks were brought to a halt and destroyed by this method. As a Generalfeldmarschall in 1945, von Greim was to be the last commander of the Luftwaffe.

The most successful example of the new German methods was a scene that took place on 21 March 1918, when the Schlachtstaffeln (ground-attack squadrons) began to support the storm troopers on the ground who had already infiltrated and bypassed what remained of the British front lines. On the other hand it was British ground-strafing attacks in their turn, that were ultimately to play a role in bringing the German onrush to a halt. Even so, some forty miles had been gained by the German army in a week in a war in which it took months to advance a few thousand yards, and the success of the German technique was there for all to ponder.

When it came time for the British to counterattack on the western front much study had been made of the German technique. Major General J.F.C. Fuller was a particularly farsighted officer, and on 24 May 1918 he produced a battle plan for ending the war the next year, Plan 1919. The plan's whole rationale was built around a strong striking force of "Medium D" tanks supported by strafing aircraft from the newly formed RAF penetrating through the German front and wiping out their Main HQ. He called this initial group the "Disorganizing Force." Once the prime objective had been achieved, a main attacking force of heavy tanks with strong air support and backing infantry was to take advantage of the confusion in the enemy rear to shatter their front and then keep moving for at least 150 miles in continual harassing pursuit. Fuller later modified the infantry's role to make them equally as mobile by moving them in trucks which would be towed by the tanks over the trenches and then would keep up with the advance.

Fuller's plan was never carried out, but the kernel of his brainchild resurfaced in the 1920s and 1930s and parts of it were adapted by other great military thinkers of that time, notably British Captain Sir Basil Liddell Hart (whose theories were ignored by his own countrymen) and German General Heinz Guderian (whose ideas were later to be put into practice in 1940).

What the British did achieve was more limited in concept but it proved effective against the now exhausted Germans who were once more on the defensive. The British method was demonstrated during the Battle of Amiens which commenced on 8 August 1918. Almost the entire strength of the British tank force (324 heavy and 96 light tanks) was secretly assembled for this one attack, again the emphasis on concentration of force. A large number of fighter squadrons was again allocated to the purely ground-attack role after their comrades had established total air superiority over the front. Another essential prerequisite of close support, the need for specialized aircraft for the task, was demonstrated here.

The Royal Air Force's strafing squadrons were assigned their own targets, which for the first time included the specific elimination of German artillery batteries along the line of advance. They were then to substitute for British heavy guns in the follow-up operations of the breakout. Thus was the era of "flying artillery" first initiated by the British. Unfortunately the "cavalry mind" still ran the British army, even after four years of trench warfare. Instead of the light tanks being given the freedom to roam at will behind the enemy lines and cause havoc, the whole of the Cavalry Corps was also sent in to work with the tanks. The horse soldiers merely got in the way and hindered the tanks, which were forced to rescue them when they ran into opposition and escort them back to British lines when the horses themselves became too weary. This was obviously not the full commitment to mobile warfare that was required. The British army had gone some of the way but in the final sweep it proved as conservative as the RAF, which was *still* refusing to organize specialized squadrons even though it allocated the fighter strafers particular targets.

Ground-strafing in the approved British manner was conducted by the American fliers when they eventually got to the western front. Under Colonel William Mitchell they delivered a set piece example of army cooperation during the battle of the St. Michel salient in September 1918. The American flyers conducted low-level strafing attacks in support of their infantry most effectively. Mitchell was, at this stage of his career, an enthusiast for close-support tactics and had worked out a comprehensive scheme employing 1,500 aircraft which, once they had gained air superiority over the target area, were committed to working closely with the advancing Doughboys.

The accuracy of low-level attacks by fighters dropping bombs left a great deal to be desired and the pilots and squadrons were largely left to their own devices on how to improve it. Independently many other British scout pilots came upon the system first used in action by Lieutenant

Generalfeldmarschall Robert Ritter von Greim (NSFK), last Supreme Commander of the Luftwaffe, pictured here in 1944. As a young Oberleutant during World War I von Greim had been among the first "tank-busting" air aces, and he had won the *pour le Mérite* for such exploits. He thus preceded Hans-Ulrich Rudel, who gained outstanding fame a quarter of a century later. Von Greim's historic close-support missions were carried out by the 34 (Bavarian) Jagdstafel in the Somme area on 1 March 1918. (Bundesarchiv-Militarchiv, Freiburg)

Above
The Nieuport 28 (seen here lovingly restored in every detail) was used by the United States Army Air Corps toward the end of World War I and made strafing attacks during the victorious American assault on the St. Michel salient on the western front in 1918. (Author's collection)

Below
The world's first combat dive-bomber pilot, Second Lieutenant William "Harry" Brown of the Royal Flying Corps (fourth from the left) is seen here with his fellow pilots of No. 84 Squadron. In a classic near-vertical bombing attack with his Se5 aircraft, against a group of German ammunition barges in northern France on 14 March 1918, Harry sank one with a direct hit. (RAF Museum, Hendon, London)

Harry Brown of 84 Squadron, an attack in a vertical dive. Several of the Sopwith Camel—equipped squadrons also found that this aircraft was particularly excellent in delivering its bomb load at the end of a steep dive. This method greatly helped the pilots in keeping their objective directly in view throughout the approach period. Because the trajectory of the released bomb was almost vertical, maximum hits were ensured on even the smallest target. Thus in 1917 on the western front was born the dive-bomber, and it was to have an overwhelming effect on close air support in the decades that followed.

Not surprisingly it was away from the mud and wire of the western front, in combat zones that were more flexible due to environment and lesser concentration of forces, that the role of the aircraft in deciding the outcome of land battles was most potently demonstrated by the RAF.

The final victorious advance of General Sir Edmund Allenby's army up the coast of Palestine commenced in September 1918. The Turkish defense line had been established by the German General Erich von Falkenhayn, and it ran from the Mediterranean coast just north of Jaffa and eastward across the Judean Hills to the Jordan River just above the Dead Sea. Three Turkish armies held this line. The 8th was closest to the coast with its headquarters at Tul Karm while the 7th held the mountainous center sector with its headquarters at the town of Nablus. Midway between Tul Karm and Nablus was the railhead town of Mas'udiye from which ran the main Turkish supply link back via the main telephone exchange at Afula to their General HQ at Nazareth in the north. The third enemy force, 4th Turkish army, was stationed astride the Jordan.

On 19 September Allenby feinted to the right and then delivered his main flanking attacks up the coast, striking directly at Nazareth but also sending columns out to cut the Turkish armies off from their bases by both taking Mas'udiye and crossing the rail link at Jenin to the north to reach the Jordan River at Beyt Shean. Both the 7th and the reinforced 4th armies found themselves trapped. It was a bold plan and one that worked to perfection.

Air power was predominant in the execution of this classic victory. The 7th and 8th Army HQs were bombed and strafed early on, and the Afula exchange was taken out at the same time. German CO Liman von Sanders was thus cut off from his armies and lost control of the battle at the critical juncture. Moreover the RAF flyers contributed much to the disintegration of the 8th Army when they caught its columns pulling back from Tul Karm to Mas'udiye. This lesson in air power was bad enough for the Turks, but worse was to follow.

Although the Turkish escape route was already in the hands of British cavalry units, communication had been reestablished with the 7th

Army and von Sanders's last orders before he himself was forced into undignified flight in his pajamas were for that still intact force to extract itself from the trap by way of the road through the Wadi Fara'a defile. Not yet directly menaced, this Turkish column was a coherent force, but it was not to remain so for long.

At first light on 21 September a mass of some 90 horse-drawn field guns and limbers, 92 supply wagons, and 55 motor trucks, was found wending its way through the narrow valley by an early reconnaissance flight. At once the whole weight of the RAF's ground-attacking squadrons were thrown against the Turkish column. These squadrons were equipped mainly with some Bristol I "Brisfits," five squadrons of SE5a fighters, and a few de Havilland D.H.9a "Ninak" light bombers.

The first strikes hit the head of the column at the beginning of a narrow defile. Once halted, the rest of the convoy was unable to get past the burning vehicles at the front and were trapped. The RAF strafers were merciless. Flying in relays, the aircraft attacked in waves, with a pair of

One of the very first examples of how tactical close air support could dominate a land battle and create total havoc in an opposing army was demonstrated by the RAF some twenty-two years before the blitzkrieg. The location of this historic air massacre was the Nablus-Beisan road in Palestine, where a retreating Turkish army was trapped in the narrow passes by wave after wave of strafing and bombing RAF fighter-bombers. The results were salutary and complete. Strangely, the powerful impression of this scene of desolation failed to influence the British air chiefs of the period between the wars, who became totally obsessed with the illusion of the strategic heavy bomber winning wars unaided. This photo shows the abandoned Turkish transports being cleared off the road on 20 September 1918. (Imperial War Museum, London)

planes machine-gunning the column every three minutes and being rein-forced by a further six machines every half-hour. This rain of destruction was kept up continually for four solid hours. At the end of that time the Turkish artillerymen had become nothing more than "a dispersed horde of trembling individuals, hiding for their lives."[3]

On the same day and in the same manner the Bulgarian army was caught retreating through the Kosturino Pass in Macedonia and slaughtered.

Finally, between 29 and 30 October 1918, in the aftermath of the battle of Vitterio Venecio, the Austro-Hungarian armies were similarly caught on the move by the RAF on the Conegliano-Pordanone road.

In the immediate aftermath of World War I there came general stag-nation in the further development and application of the lessons that the war had taught. Naturally enough in the wake of such carnage, "the War to end all War" left the populace weary of all things military. Sincere

The Sopwith Salamander was the first RAF aircraft designed with the ground-attack role in mind from the beginning. As such it was armored against small-arms fire from the engine cowling to beyond the pilot's cockpit of the fuselage. Despite its early lead in such techniques, the RAF grew more and more disenchanted with this form of attack between the two world wars because anything to do with army cooperation seemed to the RAF of that time to smack of "subservience" to the older military branches. (RAF Museum, Hendon, London)

efforts were made by well-meaning men throughout the decade that followed to seek an end to wars by treaty. Armament budgets for most democratic nations were cut to the bone. Close air support was essentially an action-initiated field. The opportunities to put into practice and improve on existing experience were extremely limited.

Study was also made difficult by attitudes. The "Independent Air Force" created in Great Britain was dominated by men so obsessed with the strategic bomber concept that they would consider no other. This led to a general neglect of any form of cooperation with the army, for in the eyes of such blinkered men cooperation meant being subservient and this they were determined not to be. Just as the army largely turned their backs on the tank and thankfully returned to their horses, so the RAF put close air support in a box and threw away the key. General Sir Edmund Ironside was to lament many years later that "Between the wars the former cooperation between the army and the air force, close, intimate and effective in the Great War, ceased when the air force became a separate force."[4]

The only concession the RAF made to the army was the development of a series of light bombers specially designed to work with troops on the ground in colonial policing campaigns. Their role was not to attack directly in conjunction with troops but merely to perform tactical reconnaissance duties, targeting artillery and dropping messages. So the British interpretation of army cooperation resulted in general purpose (GP) aircraft of which the uninspired Westland Wapiti, Wallace and Lysander, Hawker Hector and Audax, Vickers Vincent, and Fairey IIIF were typical mundane examples. But their role was by no stretch of the imagination "close air support," and all such considerations were frowned upon.

16

The French followed an almost identical pattern of stagnation, but their condition was made worse by the appalling state of the French aircraft industry. Political apathy in Britain was matched by political chaos across the Channel as governments changed with bewildering rapidity, as did their policies. The French army retained control of their aircraft, which should have aroused the interest of the Aviation Militaire in the furtherance of close support, but the "Maginot" mentality, of reliance on rigid, fixed underground defense lines, spread throughout its whole structure. Thus aggressive use of military air power had no place in a system that was completely geared to a totally static defense scenario for two decades.

Again, apart from colonial policing and the experience of the Moroccan "Rif" wars in the 1920s (when dive-bombing was recognized as having the greatest potential for supporting troop due to its accuracy against small targets), the defense-minded French attitude produced nothing but Multiplace de Combat airplane designs. These aircraft were capable of doing many tasks, but were mediocre at them all. The French concepts hinged on aircraft like the Breguet XIX series which were developments of the existing XIV type. They lingered on in various forms and with various power plants for fifteen years! The type was also widely exported.

The third of the great wartime democracies was the United States. It had failed to develop its own military aviation and had been dependent on British and French expertise and designs. The end of the war found it with vast numbers of brand-new Boeing DH-4 aircraft on its hands whose design was obsolete compared with the current European types. Refitting them with the new Liberty engine gave them an extended life-span. As the United States withdrew from the world stage into isolationism, opportunities to extend the knowledge of close-support operations

Early French experiments in the ground-attack role featured the Breguet Type XVI BN2 night bomber, here seen fitted with underwing racks and carrying both light and medium bombs. Notice also the siren carried on the strut above the lower wing, an early version of the Stuka's notorious "Trombones of Jericho" used to such good effect many years later. This standard bomber of World War I proved very successful in combat. (SHAA, Paris)

that they had assimilated in France in 1917–18 were few and limited in scope.

Like Britain and France, the United States' war experience was confined to aerial policing actions. They had no colonies, of course, but the application of the Monroe Doctrine meant that they kept order in those areas of the Americas they considered essential, and so intervention was sanctioned in Mexico, Haiti, and Nicaragua. The three examples mentioned did involve air and ground forces working closely together, albeit on a small scale, and were important for that reason. As a side effect, these operations also acted as a catalyst in the conversion of the United States Marine Corps, and ultimately the US Navy, to the dive-bombing concept. In time, the US interest in dive-bombing also aroused the interest of General Ernst Udet of Germany, which would have a vast impact upon close air support.

The United States' Air and Cavalry Punitive Expedition into Mexico in 1919 has received little attention but is deserving of record here as one of the first occasions that aircraft worked with cavalry in the postwar period. An earlier expedition in 1916–17 under "Black Jack" Pershing to bring Pancho Villa to heel was a fiasco, with the air component losing all its aircraft and achieving nothing.

The 1919 campaign was a smaller affair and the aircraft involved mainly confined themselves to reconnaissance for the troopers. One noteworthy contribution was made on 19 August when a DH-4 flown by Lieutenant F. S. Estill, with Lieutenant R. H. Cooper as his observer-gunner, was scouting ahead of the 8th Cavalry. They were searching a canyon in the Tinaja Verde region when they spotted three of the bandits on horseback, who fired at the aircraft. Lieutenant Estill banked and made a low pass over the horsemen, opening fire with his synchronized Marlin machine guns, which fired directly ahead through his prop, while Lieutenant Cooper gave the bandits a burst with his twin Lewis as they passed. They hit and killed one man who was later found to be the bandit leader Jesus Rentria.

Aside from that, the work of the United States Air Service squadrons' aircraft, twelve from 20 Aero Squadron and six from 11 Aero Squadron, which all belonged to 1 Bombardment Group under Major E. G. Tobin, was described thus by Major James P. Yancey:

> The airplanes worked well with the troops and furnished valuable information as to the movements of Mexican troops, located water and camping places, and furnished a quick means of communication with Headquarters at Marfa. Much was learned by both branches regarding cooperation and the needs of each other.

Observers made sketches of country in our front and dropped them to us. Pilots would locate water, then come and circle our Column and fly directly to the water and circle. Message bags furnished a good means of communication from air to ground.[5]

Such a description could be given for a dozen similar actions carried out by the British and French air forces at this period, from the northwest frontier of India to Iraq and the Rif Mountains. It was not close support in the true sense of the word. Nonetheless credit must be given to the men of the Border Patrol for keeping the concept alive. When aviator "Turk" Tourtellot visited 3 Attack Group under the command of Major Louis H. Brereton at that time he found them operating their DH-4s with ten external Mark A-III bomb racks fixed under the wings and bomb release switches installed in the cockpits. They were utilizing the dive-bombing method with eye-sighting only in practice attacks. They employed attack angles of between 60 and 70 degrees despite the fact that the old DH was neither built nor stressed for such delivery.

Marine Corps pilots' work in Haiti in 1919 against the "Caco" rebels in the heavily jungled interior was different in some respects and flown during actual combat conditions.

The aircraft used were DH-4Bs of 4 Air Squadron commanded by Captain Harvey B. Mims. None of these machines was fitted with bombsights, and attacks made in the low-level configuration had not proven satisfactory. Lieutenant S. H. Sanderson rigged up a makeshift bomb carrier out of a canvas mail bag and tied it below the fuselage of his machine with a bomb in it and with a drag rope leading to the cockpit. He attacked the rebels in a shallow dive and released the bomb at a height of 250 feet by tugging the rope. This has frequently (and ludicrously) been described by air historians as the origin of dive bombing! Although this plainly is not the case, it *did* reintroduce the use of bombing from the air to assist troops on the ground in difficult terrain.

The United States Navy was also dedicated to the concept of using its fighter aircraft in low-level approaches against enemy troops. In 1925 Captain Joseph Mason Reeves assumed command of Aircraft Battle Force and, in the summer of the following year, concentrated all Pacific fleet aircraft at North Island, San Diego, to develop type tactics and joint tactics for the various types of aircraft. One of the squadrons concerned was VF-2 equipped with Curtiss F6C fighters. Admiral F. D. Wagner has left this interesting firsthand account:

Among the questions propounded by then Captain Reeves to the fighters was "How to repel a landing force endeavoring to land on a beach?" Strafing was the obvious answer because histories of air activities in World War I were replete with instances of the complete rout and dispersal of troops when they were attacked by low-flying planes strafing with machine guns. Light fragmentation bombs were also dropped by aircraft in their attacks on ground forces.

In answering Captain Reeves' questions we started out with the tactics used in World War I, that is, low flying and strafing targets off North Island with machine gun fire. Hitting accuracy was very poor because in a flat glide or level flying the targets disappeared from view at close range. Furthermore, with the development of semi-automatic anti-aircraft guns, it appeared that aircraft would have little opportunity of reaching their target.[6]

Wagner's flyers thought they had discovered not only the answer to the problem but a whole new concept of air attack when they used the dive-bombing method. Their tactics were to make an approach above 10,000 feet and then to make converging dives at angles of 70 degrees plus onto the target.

In fact, of course, the US Navy flyers had merely rediscovered the dive-bombing technique the RAF used in combat in 1917 and discarded after extensive trials at the Orfordness testing grounds.

Further combat was seen by the US Marine Corps, which included a Marine air contingent, in Nicaragua against the Moncada rebels, who were threatening to overthrow the Diaz regime. What followed in 1927 was a major milestone in American cooperation between ground and air forces. Major Ross Rowell's VO-1M with six DH-4s were soon in action against the enemy forces at Octal, where a small Marine force was cut off and threatened by a large number of Augusto Sandoni's rebel forces.

Reinforced by VO-4-M, and later equipped with the new ground-attack aircraft, the Vought O2U-1 Corsair, Rowell and his flyers proved invaluable. Low-level strafing attacks with both machine guns and small 25-pound fragmentation bombs were conducted. Later attacks utilizing the larger 50-pound demolition bombs were carried out against the rebel stronghold at San Albino. Four Corsairs were employed, attacking in two pairs in near-vertical dives.

As a result of all this combat and study, the US Navy became sold on dive bombing, while the US Army Air Corps veered more and more toward the British and French concept of ground strafing. Both services, however, were more aware than these two European air forces of the need for specialized aircraft to fulfill their respective needs. This awareness brought the arrival in the navy of dive bombers like Curtiss O2C-1 Helldiver and the development for the army of ground-strafing types like the Douglas O-2. One of the latter was adapted by fitting six fixed, forward-firing .303 Browning machine guns in addition to the two flexible Lewis guns in the cockpits. Armor protection was fitted to the engine, cooling system, and under the cockpit itself against ground fire.

Further US Army Air Corps (USAAC) developments followed along these lines, with the Curtiss A-3 Falcon (the *A* standing for attack—the new category emphasizing the increasing status close-support aircraft were beginning to have in the service). A technical advance over the normal biplane types was the Curtiss A-12 Shrike, which had the distinction of being the first American military aircraft designed specifically for the ground-attack role. A single-engine machine, it featured a fixed undercarriage with heavy "spats" which housed a Browning machine gun. Additional machine guns were fixed in the wings for low-level strafing attack, and it could also carry 500 pounds of bombs.

Japan's navy and army also continued to control their respective air arms, like the United States but unlike the British and Italians. Two Japanese army officers had been sent to Europe to train as aviators as early as 1910, Captain Yoshitoshi Tokugawa to France and Captain Kumazo Hino to Germany. Indeed, Captain Tokugawa of the Imperial Army had later designed the first aircraft to be built exclusively in Japan.

Although a home-based aircraft industry was long established, it was still dependent largely on imported ideas and technology. A British aviation mission under Lord Sempill arrived in the 1920s charged with training and advising the Japanese in aviation matters (the two nations were still bound by treaty at this time). They found a good basic setup and pupils willing and eager to learn all they could. The role of the close-support aircraft was not one of the principal lessons imparted, however, due to its eclipse in Britain itself, and so the Japanese had to find the need for such aircraft from their own experiences.

In 1920 Japanese military flyers had been involved in incidents at Vladivostok, but only as observers. Following the formation of the army air corps in 1925, the Tsinan Incident in China again demonstrated the need for rugged types of aircraft suited for front-line duties to assist ground forces in primitive conditions. While it is a fact that the Imperial Navy was not slow in learning and copying the development of the dive bomber from its main rivals across the Pacific, again this did not involve close-support operations ashore.

The other major European power was Italy. Italy had witnessed the power of strafing aircraft firsthand but was plagued with a wretched economy. The advent of Benito Mussolini and his Fascist regime heralded an increasing emphasis on nationalism and expansion of military power. The Regia Aeronautica shared the vision of strategic bombers lay-

This 1920s RAF Sopwith Snipe with twelve light bombs on racks below the fuselage and under each wing shows what was meant by antipersonnel firepower during those years. This aircraft is of No. 25 squadron, RAF, based at Hawkinge in Kent at this period. (RAF Museum, Hendon, London)

ing waste to whole cities, but more practical considerations led to the adaptation of general-purpose army-support aircraft along the lines of British planes. A typical manifestation of this commitment was to be found in the Stormi da Bombardamento concept. Examples of this were the Caproni Ca101 "Colonial" all-purpose and attack aircraft, and more pertinently the later Meridionali Ro-37, a two-seater biplane built for reconnaissance, light bombing, and cooperative work.

Set apart from all these major nations, both politically and militarily, was the great enigma of the Soviet Union. Blessed with endless manpower, their traditional military machine, the Russian steamroller, was like a dinosaur: huge, capable of withstanding endless casualties and still being able to come back for more. Able to surrender enormous areas of land without being overrun, it had always been infantry-oriented. Air power had not played a great part in the campaigns of the Great War but, on 7 November 1917, the revolutionary government inherited some 2,500 aircraft of all types.

Unlike the other major powers, the coming of peace in 1918 did not include the Russians. They were still involved in a bitter civil war, "Red" Bolsheviks against the "White" forces of the former Imperial supporters. In addition to that, many of its subjugated nations took their chance to throw off the chains of Muscovy and declare their independence: Finland, Estonia, Lithuania, Latvia, and, for a time, Georgia and the Ukraine. Nor was this all; counterrevolutionaries had to be dealt with— witness the ruthless crushing of a mutiny in the Baltic fleet at Kronstadt in March 1921, when thirty Red Air Fleet machines bombed and strafed the sailors in support of 7 Red Army's assault.

Continuous fighting therefore impelled the newly formed Communist state to improve and adjust on its feet, merely to survive. Under Leon

Trotsky a great Red Army was created which, like the Revolutionary army of France in the 1790s, astounded the world by beating off all challengers. In conjunction with this army, a number of Socialist Aviation Detachments (or *Aviadarm*) were established under the Bureau of Commissars of Aviation and Aeronautics. The intense aerial fighting, coupled with the confusion of the land battles, gave rise to great wastage of aircraft. In September 1918 the Aviadarm had at their disposal only 315 front-line aircraft and these were mainly license-built types like French Caudron, Farmans and Nieuports 17 and 23s, and British Sopwith 1 1/2 Strutters, all semiobsolete.

One of the bitterest of the little wars was that fought with Poland. The Poles had managed to get hold of two hundred war-surplus German aircraft. These were placed at the disposal of Marshal Pilduski's army, which set off east to expand the boundaries of the new state as far as their cavalry formations could penetrate while the Russians were at each other's throats.

In the wide open spaces beyond the Pripet marshes it was difficult to establish set lines of defense, and the aircraft could be moved around the battle fronts to give maximum effect. Here the Poles laid the cornerstone of their future air policy, the importance of *liniowe* (front-line) aircraft for close support of armies in the field. From this experience they created specialized machines for the job. It proved difficult for the aircraft and their supporting ground crews and materials to keep up with the advance while using poor lines of communication. At the front line such essential items as aircraft spares and fuel became virtually nonexistent. As a result of this lack of transport, the Polish air-support aircraft began to drop by the wayside.

After not too many weeks the Soviets had organized their resistance to the Polish invasion. In July 1920 deputy head I. A. Buob had managed to assemble some 51 flights with a total of 210 aircraft to support Marshal Mikhail Tukhachevski's counterattack. Like the Poles before them, the Soviets found that keeping the flow of supplies, fuel, and spares to the combat units in the field was a difficult task. Also, the Red Air Force suffered from the lack of sufficiently trained aircrew because the officer class had largely sided with the White forces. Nonetheless, the aviators contributed much to the counteradvance, which took them to the gates of Warsaw itself.

The Poles were saved by two factors. The Soviets had overreached themselves, and the French intervened on the side of the Poles. France dispatched General Maxime Weygand with a military mission that included a large air component, including Bristol fighters and similar machines which they used to support the Polish armies in the field. With this support the Poles staged an impressive comeback, driving the Soviet armies back to the old frontiers once more. Both sides were by now exhausted and a peace treaty was finally signed in October 1920.

In Poland the result of this experience was that their military aviation branch, the Lotnictwo Wojskowe, made the construction of ground-attack aircraft a priority, initially with imported planes like the Breguet XIX, but also with their home-built Potez XXV and XXVI biplanes. In Russia similar lessons had been drawn, and although long-range bombers were important before the revolution, the main emphasis in the 1920s and 1930s was on close-support aviation, which the Soviets were to bring to a fine art.

In September 1923 the Red Air Force was reorganized around a basic unit of three machines, which the Russians called *zveno*. There were also squadrons (*eskadrilya*), and air groups (*aviagruppa*) as aircraft units in the Soviet Air Force. Because Tukhachevski believed in the tank and in armored formation attack, his influence was concentrated in producing a suitable ground-attack aircraft to support the tanks and act with them. The need for a close-support air weapon was never in doubt, and much thought and design work went into producing one. Four different prototypes for a future Shturmovik bomber were produced by the design bureau, all based on the existing R-5 aircraft, but all were deemed inadequate. A twin-engine design was put forward by aircraft designer Andrei Tupolev but this was also rejected. Finally designers M. I. Gurevich and S. A. Kocherigin put forward the Tsh-3 design, an advanced concept of a heavily armored low-wing monoplane.

In the end, while design work continued, vast numbers of close-support machines were obtained by the simple expedient of converting existing types and adding protection. The two main types used, both two-seater biplanes, were thus employed. The DI-6 was a simple adaptation of a standard two-seater fighter. More in keeping with what was desired was the Polikarpov R-5Sh, which was converted from the R-5 by the addition of armor and four extra machine guns below the wings. An improved variant of this was the R-SSS, which had spatted wheels and four additional forward-firing ShKAS machine guns. Maximum bomb load was two 550-pounders. Both these types began to enter service early in the 1930s, by which time close-support aviation was at the beginning of a complete rebirth and reassessment as the world began lurching, with increasing rapidity, toward another world war.

three

Theories and Practice

The decade between 1929 and the outbreak of World War II saw the most significant advances in the design and performance of aircraft. In those ten years speeds more than doubled, biplanes and wires-and-struts gave way (except in a few backward air forces) to monoplanes, hand-held machine guns evolved into multiple fixed and turret weapons, and engine performance (both in-line and radial) increased enormously. Although this was all reflected in the state of the art of the aircraft used in the ground-attack role, the method itself, and its application, remained a relatively neglected area of study and enterprise until the mid 1930s. During these years the expansionist powers, Italy, Japan, and then Germany, began using force to back up their arguments. Of course the Soviet Union had never adopted any other stance and continued to improve on it, while the lesser nations merely began falling in line. The campaigns of aggression (by Italy in Abyssinia and by Japan in China, coupled with Japan's contretemps with the Soviets in Manchuria and finally the intervention on both sides in Spain) reconfirmed the vital role that air power could play in helping an army make conquests both quickly and economically.

As always, the aggressor nations, initiating and utilizing the experiments and conducting the live actions, benefited most and applied the lessons most diligently. Thus the practical proof of the effectiveness of tactical air power was made part and parcel of these nations' armories

The perfection of the standard light bomber between the wars was epitomized in the Hawker Hart two-seater shown here, which first flew in 1928, entered squadron service in 1930, and spawned a whole host of variants: the Audax for army cooperation, the Hardy for general-purpose duties, the improved Hind, and the Hector, used by the RAF in June 1940 as a dive-bomber because they had nothing else. (RAF Museum, Hendon, London)

The US Marine Corps was in the forefront of developing the concept of close-support air power in the lean years of the 1920s and 1930s. By the middle of that period both US Navy and Marine Corps aviators had taken a firm stand on the dive-bombing concept as the most accurate and cost-effective means of delivering heavy ordnance by air exactly on target, both at sea and in land operations. The ultimate biplane expression of the dive-bomber in America finalized with the Curtiss SBC-4 "Helldiver." A Marine Corps example is shown here. (US National Archives, Washington, DC)

and thinking, while the hesitant democracies, Britain, France, and the United States, tended to cling longest to their much-cherished theories of strategical bombing, which had never been put to the acid test of combat. None of the aggressor states required long-range aircraft to fulfill their ambitions, for all sought merely to expand by the step-by-step absorption and conquest of neighboring lands. As long as they could take on their chosen victims one or two at a time, tactical bombing in support of their armies suited the bill perfectly. To criticize the Germans' military planning for lacking a long-range bomber design in 1937, when all they wanted was adjacent parts of Europe, is to use hindsight based upon the totally unforeseen conditions of 1943. What would have been the use of a heavy bomber capable of reaching Moscow or New York to a war command that wanted only to take Prague or Warsaw?

Not only was this credibility gap obvious between countries, it was also apparent between different services in the same country. The gap was just as wide between the concepts held by the naval air arms of both Great Britain and the United States and their opposite numbers in the RAF and USAAC. In 1937 the differing attitudes between the US Army fliers on one hand and the US Navy and Marine Corps fliers on the other, were summed up in this manner.

> Low-altitude dive bombing from scout and observation airplanes armed with light fragmentation bombs was practiced by the Marine Corps in some of their small wars operations as early as 1927. Naval aviation began experiments with dive-bombing fighters about the same time. The present development of high-altitude, high-speed dive bombing began, however, with the advent of the Curtiss Helldiver in 1930. This airplane was the forerunner of the present type heavy dive bomber, and was instrumental in the formulation of dive-bombing technique and tactics, as practiced by [American] naval aviation today.
>
> The [Army] Air Corps has conducted some dive-bombing experiments with pursuit airplanes in recent years, but has never evolved any tactics for the employment of dive bombers as a class. At present there are no airplanes within the army air forces capable of being used as dive bombers.
>
> Dive bombers are of particular tactical value against precision and manuevering [sic] targets. The radius of action, and the tactics employed for this class of bombardment aviation, are analogous to those prescribed by the Air Corps for attack units.

In considering the practicability of adoption by the army air forces of dive bombing there were four principal considerations.

> 1. Tactical adaptability for army missions. The army air forces today are lacking a weapon for the precision bombing of small, important targets, heavily defended by machine-gun fire, and of such a nature as to require bombs of medium size. The conventional bomber lacks the requisite accuracy, and the attack

plane cannot carry the necessary bomb load. The dive bomber is the proper weapon in this case.

2.   Influence on bombing accuracy. Dive bombing reduces the bombing error by half, and is therefore four times as effective as the horizontal bomber carrying the same bomb load. A squadron of single-motor dive bombers similar in size to the A-17 is equal by reason of this superior accuracy to the same number of B-17 bombers within the range capabilities of the smaller airplanes.

3.   Comparative security from antiaircraft fire. There appears to be no essential advantage in favor of either type. Both will suffer casualties when they operate at their most effective altitude for bombing accuracy; and against heavily defended objectives those casualties will be severe. A flight of dive bombers costs approximately the same as one B-17, and carries about the same personnel. Although the percentage in loss of units will be the same, the loss in men and material from the horizontal bombing units is six times that of the dive bombing squadron. [This was because the heavy bombers were larger machines, much more expensive, and carried seven or eight crew members as against only two in the navy dive bombers.]

4.   Performance limitations. Considering the most recently developed dive bomber, there appears to be no sacrifice of performance for strength. The A-17 is an excellent tactical airplane, and its counterpart in a dive bomber should be acceptable to the army air forces. Whether multi-engine craft of larger size and range can be successfully employed as dive bombers is problematical, and it would seem more conservative at present to accept a radius of action for dive bombers commensurate with the performance characteristics of the A-17. This is ample for operations in support of ground forces. . . .

The final recommendations were:

A.   That the Air Corps procure appropriate numbers of the new design dive bombers. . . .

B.   That pursuit airplanes be equipped with bomb racks for dive bombing operations. . . .

C.   That Air Corps pilots be trained in the technique and tactics of dive bombing.

D.   That initially, the dive bombers be assigned to attack units in the ratio of one dive bombing squadron per group. Because of the present similarity of airplanes this would facilitate operation and maintenance; and would permit proper utilization of the tactical analogy existing between the two types.[1]

In fact, the air corps was happy with the A-17 as it was. What it required at this period was a simple, strong, and reliable airplane that could minister to the needs of the ground forces as a close-support auxiliary machine. This single-engine, low-wing monoplane had a fixed, spatted undercarriage just like the German Junkers "Stuka" and the Japanese Aichi "Val," but it had been designed and stressed merely as a ground strafer and light bomber, not for dive-bombing. Its armament of four forward-firing .303 machine guns, plus another for rearward defense, was considered sufficient at this time when pursuit biplanes mounted only a pair of such weapons. The US Army ordered no less than 110 of them at a total cost of two million dollars, an enormous sum for that time. They first entered service in 1937 and Northrop won major export orders with developments of this type to China, Sweden, Peru, the Netherlands, Iraq, and Argentina.

A similar advanced single-engine monoplane had been produced by the Vultee company in 1935. It could carry 600 pounds of bombs and had four forward-firing Browning machine guns for strafing. Although it found little favor at home, other nations found it to their liking and it was sold to the Soviet Union, China, Turkey, and Brazil as the V-11 and the V-12.

The army air corps meanwhile continued to upgrade its requirements for attack aircraft. The needs were for ever heavier bomb loads and machine guns, but still the payload had to be delivered at low level. The Curtiss company came up with one answer with their A-18 Shrike. The A-18 was a twin-engine design to give the aircraft the power required to take into battle a 654-pound bomb load carried internally and four .303 Browning machine guns mounted in its pencil-slim nose.

When this aircraft appeared, its revolutionary design caused a great sensation. Also, it was 20 mph faster than the standard air corps pursuit machine, the Boeing P-26. Such a combination should have proven unbeatable, but the Curtiss Shrike, as it was named, flopped. The underlying American need was for a fast aircraft capable of fighting its way through to the target, delivering its bomb load and contributing its strafing fire to the army's advance, and still being able to hold its own in combat with any hostile fighter defenses. Such a combination was to be proved impossible time and again, but in the mid 1930s this impossible demand stretched the US aircraft industry to its limits. Only thirteen A-18s were finally ordered due to budget limitations and these went to the 8th Attack Squadron in 1940.

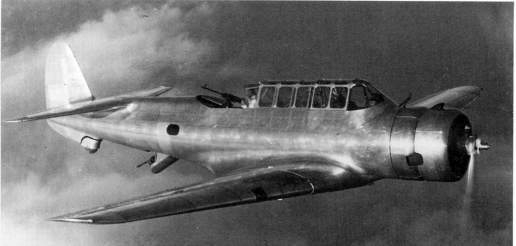

Above
The visually pleasing Northrop Model-2 light attack bomber followed a series of mail planes like the Gamma and Delta concepts that brought aerodynamic advances to a new high in the United States in the mid-1930s. The USAAC approved the basic airframe, which at that time included the fixed undercarriage as shown here, but specified the fitting of the aircraft with the 750-horsepower Pratt & Whitney R-1535 engine. One hundred and ten of these aircraft joined the service as the A-17. (Smithsonian Institution, Washington, DC)

Below
The Vultee V-12 of the late 1930s was the state of the art in American thinking for single-engine light attack bombers. Embodying all the latest techniques in construction and the low-wing form of the highly successful mail aircraft of the period, the V-12 failed to make the grade in the US but was purchased widely abroad in such countries as China and Turkey. (Smithsonian Institution, Washington, DC)

The final prewar development of the logical progression of the USAAC's attack aviation ideas was the Douglas A-20. The original concept was reconceived in 1936 as a twin-engine aircraft with four heavy machine guns mounted in the nose and an internal bomb bay. By the time this basic design had been modified and flown in October 1938, the army had moved on from the attack concept to the light bomber concept prevailing elsewhere. Nonetheless, with a large number of modifications, the type found favor with the French as a ground-attack machine, the DB-7, and later in a wide variety of conventional roles with other Allied air forces including Britain's and the Soviet Union's.

Developed in 1940 from the A-20 was the Douglas A-26 Invader or Havoc. It featured the same high-shoulder wings and twin-engine design as the A-20 but it was not a one-mission aircraft. Instead the Havoc was designed from the outset to fulfill a multimission profile. By that time the war in Europe had provided the army air corps with a whole new set of examples and had triggered some massive thinking and rethinking.

Although American aircraft designs in this period were revolutionary in concept and bold in execution, the more practical needs of the troops on the ground were being filled by European air forces both large and small with applications of old and largely forgotten principles now being rediscovered.

Sweden's small air force, the *Flygvapnet*, for example, was built for the sole purpose of ground attack in support of the army. With a small population and restricted defense, their thinking was that every bomb must count. Mass-area bombing never featured in their air strategy, therefore, but precision bombing on specific targets in close proximity to their ground forces was considered essential. They were early in the rediscovery of the importance of dive-bombing in this respect, as the following makes clear.

> The first planned Swedish trials with dive-bombing attacks were held in Autumn 1934 by No. 4 Wing at Fröson. We can add here that an entirely independent, separate occurrence was noted at this time.
>
> A well-known test pilot from the German Junkers works at Dessau and some other personnel from that factory, with a Limhamn-assembled specialised Junkers K 47 plane, had obtained permission from the Swedish government to execute rocket-bombing tests at the air base at Fröson at the same time. The Swedish team and the German team therefore had the opportunity to observe each other's respective trials and to exchange some views. Some authors state that the German preference in the early

In Sweden license-built Hawker Harts were adapted, as the B5, for dive-bombing as well as close-support missions. They were much utilized in that role between 1936 and 1940 before being replaced by newer monoplane types, both imported and homebuilt. (Nils Kindberg, Stockholm)

stages of World War II for dive-bombing and the birth of their Stuka airplane, the Junkers Ju 87, shortly before that period, was influenced in part by the Fröson experiments of 1934.

The Swedish dive-bombing trials that year were performed with Hawker Hart light bombers purchased from the Hawker Aircraft Company of Great Britain. Later on from 1937 to 1940, licensed-built Harts were produced and these were delivered to No. 4 and No. 6 Light Bomber Wings.

The dive-bombing trials at Fröson developed so successfully that in 1935–36 they were followed by a second series at the Malmlatt Test Centre in Ostrogothia, with the aim of establishing the basic parameters of dive-bombing. These produced some clearly new features and the method became a specialty in Sweden. In 1937 training for dive-bombing was practised at a special attack course held by No. 1 Wing at Vasteras, close to Lake Malaren. The pupils were mainly senior and well-experienced pilots.[2]

In fact the Germans were already wedded to close-support aviation by the mere fact that the fledgling Luftwaffe was composed mainly of ex-army officers who naturally thought in such terms. In addition the Germans, largely disarmed after the Great War, had neither the requirement nor the basic industrial base to construct fleets of long-rang bombers on the British style. As Eberhard Spetzler quite logically pointed out, Germany in the 1930s "had no choice but to limit herself to medium and light bombers with the highest possible degree of hitting accuracy."[3]

Germany's wholehearted embracing of precision bombing was

therefore not a result of shortsightedness but of deliberate choice for both the above reasons. This thinking was clearly summed up by the German General Staff in the spring of 1938 when they stated: "The emphasis in offensive bombardment has clearly shifted from area to pin-point bombardment."[4]

These conclusions stemmed mainly from the work of the Junkers Ju 87s in Spain. The arrival of the Stuka consolidated the dedication of the Luftwaffe to army support. Of course German aircraft manufacturers had been building dive-bombers long before then and selling them to other countries because they had no official air force of their own. The Heinkel He 66Ch was a biplane dive-bomber and twelve were built for China in 1934. A second group of twenty-one produced the following year were held back for the newly revealed Luftwaffe. The He 50A fighter was being employed as a temporary dive-bomber and these joined Fliegergruppe Schwerin along with some Arado Ar 65s in October 1935.

This unit became Stukagruppe 162 in April 1936 and initially was reequipped with the Henschel Hs 123, a lively little single-engine biplane which was given combat testing in Spain in 1937. The leader of the German air contingent, Wolfram von Richthofen, was against the dive-bombing principle but much engrossed with the ground-strafing potential of the Schlachtflugzeug. Here, with the Condor Legion, the Henschel Hs 123 performed most notably in the direct-support role, despite the primitive equipment and techniques employed. The Spanish Nationalists asked for more to be sent and, at the end of its dive-bomber days in Germany, this aircraft was retained as a ground-attack (*Schlachtgruppen*) airplane and was still in combat use in World War II. Thus the arrival, in 1937, of the Junkers Ju 87A in the German dive-bomber units meant that the Luftwaffe was receiving its fourth-generation dive-bomber and *not* its first, as is still so often claimed. The He 50A also saw combat service in the latter days of World War II as a night ground-attack machine (*Nachtschlachtgruppen*) on the Baltic Coast in 1943–44.

The Italians had long been interested in mass sorties of low-flying aircraft supporting their ground forces. They used the term "grazing flight" because the aircraft almost grazed the ground. This idea was developed into their famous *Massa da Caccia* concept. In the late 1920s and throughout the 1930s one Italian unit, 5 Stormo d'Assalto, gradually perfected its tactics of massed aircraft assaults from the sky. The pilot who most believed in this concept was Colonel Amedo Mecozzi, but like most pioneers he was often derided and criticized by his own countrymen. Nor did he have the machines to demonstrate the technique to its

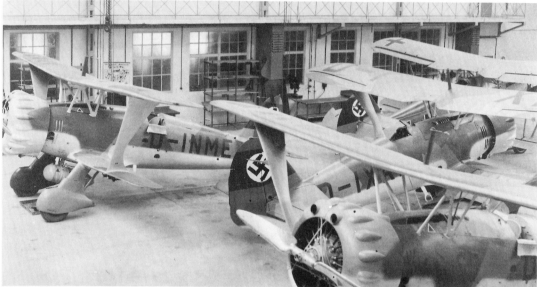

Above

Intervention by various large powers on both sides of the Spanish Civil War between 1936 and 1939 enabled these combatants to test their latest equipment under full war conditions. The Germans contributed the Legion Kondor to the fray and learned valuable lessons that came to fruition in the blitzkrieg techniques that conquered Europe only months later.

In addition to the first combat missions by the notorious Junkers Ju 87 "Stuka" dive-bombers, the German pilots used their very latest fighter aircraft—the Me 109 shown here—in ground-strafing missions at very low levels, which proved the value of such methods in demoralizing the opponent. (Bundesarchiv-Militarchiv, Freiburg)

Below

One of the first "standard" types to be adopted by Hitler's Luftwaffe in the mid-1930s for dive-bombing was the versatile and strong little Henschel Hs 123, which replaced the existing Heinkel He 50 and Arado Ar 65 types then in service. It could carry one 550-pound bomb under the fuselage and four 110-pound bombs under the wings, exactly the same payload as its successor, the famed and feared Junkers Ju 87 "Stuka." Here Hs 123s are seen at the end of the production line at the Henschel plant. The Hs 123 was powered by a 580-hp BMW 132 radial engine. Eclipsed in the dive-bombing field, the Hs 123 made a remarkable and successful comeback during the blitzkrieg and later in Russia as a ground-attack aircraft. (Peter Schwarzkopff)

A successful wartime adaptation was the Italian Caproni Cr42 fighter, which, with the addition of underwing bombs, performed well as a fighter-bomber with the Regia Aeronautica's ground-attack squadrons, the Stormo Assalto units, in the Libyan campaigns of 1941 to 1942. (Author's collection)

best effect, for most of his planes were not very good assault aircraft. The type of aircraft that the Italians utilized in developing this concept varied, but none was really outstanding. They included the Ansaldo A.C.-3, Fiat CR.20, A.P.1, Breda 64 and 65 (developed from a fighter), and finally the Breda 88 "Lince" (Lynx).

Of these aircraft, the Breda 88 was specially designed for low-altitude ground support and showed much promise on the drawing board. It was a twin-engine high-wing monoplane equipped with a fixed nose armament of three 12.7-mm Breda-SAFAT machine guns as well as two 550-pound bombs and had a speed of just over 300 mph. The use of semiobsolete fighter aircraft in the troop-support role was common to most air forces and Italy was no exception, the Fiat CR.32 being one of the first.

Nor were the Italians enamored with the dive-bomber for army cooperation work. What most appealed to them in this context was the dive-bomber's accuracy against targets like ships at sea. Mussolini was all for having a weapon that could drive the British Mediterranean fleet out of his "Mare Nostrum." Thus, although the first Italian-built dive-bomber, the Savoia Marchetti Sm 85, was designed by Alessandro Marchetti in 1935–36 and the first prototype flew on 19 December 1936 at Varese in northern Italy, application for ground attack was not its prime consideration.

In British Air Ministry circles there was a marked reluctance at all levels to take air support of the army seriously, or to consider it at all,

even in the aftermath of China and Spain. The official attitude was emphasized by Wing Commander J. C. Slessor in a series of lectures delivered at Camberley Staff College between 1931 and 1934 in which his principal theme was the airplane was not a battlefield weapon. He affirmed that the RAF considered the construction of specialized aircraft for such a role uneconomic.

Sir Maurice Dean reveals what such an attitude meant in practice in the 1930s. "In the last few years of peace there was still something called 'Army Co-operation,' a specialist art carried on, figuratively speaking, in dark corners and not taken very seriously. Venerable Audaxes had been seen picking up messages (in the notional battlefield) with sticks attached to their undercarriages. It was of course all undiluted nonsense, the tactics involved belonging to the world of fantasy."[5]

Although close air support was "undiluted nonsense" to the RAF, unfortunately the Germans were in deadly earnest. Given the differences in attitude, the debacle of May 1940 becomes less of a mystery. To the RAF dive-bombing was completely beyond the pale. One year before the Stukas began blasting the path to Warsaw, a British policy meeting held to consider dive-bombing concluded with magnificent disregard to the

A formation of Italian Breda Br65 light assault bombers here seen over a desert airfield in North Africa. Although it was designed for low-level attacks, it did achieve a limited success in the shallow dive-bombing configuration during the Spanish Civil War with the Italian intervention forces. However, it proved less suited to the more exacting combat conditions in World War II and saw only limited employment. (Nicola Malizia)

rest of the world's air forces that "steep dive bombing should not at present be regarded as a requirement for modern RAF aircraft . . . " and that "no special dive bombing armament trials are required."[6]

In truth, as Dean was forced to acknowledge, ideas on how to give the army close backup from the air were "lamentably deficient. The lessons of the First World War had been forgotten, the techniques had to be studied all over again and the period of adjustment was costly and painful."[7]

A British Air Ministry pamphlet had this to say on the subject in 1939:

> A pilot before undertaking any dive bombing training must be thoroughly proficient at flying and have complete confidence in the type of aeroplane that he is to use.
>
> The amount of training necessary to make a pilot proficient depends a great deal on the individual, some pilots requiring considerably more practice than others. It must be borne in mind that the whole essence of a successful dive bombing attack lies in the accuracy of the first bomb as in time of war only one attack may

37

be possible. It is vital, therefore, that pilots should be trained to drop their first bomb reasonably near the target and not to use it as a fighter.

It is necessary for a dive bombing pilot to be trained to judge distance on the ground accurately. This is best achieved by placing marks at certain distances from the target by which pilots can fix their aiming marks.[8]

In spite of the ministry's advice on training pilots, at the outbreak of war the RAF had no dedicated ground-attack aircraft of any type, no theory of ground attack, and no will or inclination to introduce either. The standard light bomber of the period, the Fairey Battle, was in no way suitable for the role but was merely a back-area bomber of the old type. Brief flirtations with the dive-bomber had resulted in the creation of the pleasing Hawker Henley dive-bomber by famous British aircraft designer Sidney Camm. The general scorn with which army support was increasingly held in the 1930s by the RAF relegated this dive-bomber to antiaircraft target-towing, a decision that says more about British military air policy between the wars than a thousand words!

The Royal Navy on the other hand was convinced that the dive-bomber was just what it needed, but was repeatedly frustrated in its attempts to get one. It finally had to order its own design straight from the drawing board and was forced to compromise. Instead of being a pure dive-bomber, the airplane also had to serve as a second-rate interceptor. Compromise rarely works, and the resulting aircraft, the Blackburn Skua, was a reasonably good dive-bomber, but was almost always used as a fighter. Even so there was no consideration given to supporting troops ashore, and so the naval dive-bombers of this era do not directly form a part of our story.

The same arguments raged in France but here L'Armée de l'Air concentrated on producing ground-strafing aircraft rather than dive-bombers, although, on the eve of war, it did place large orders for dive-bombers with the United States. The aircraft with which it equipped its tactical squadrons gradually improved but there were never enough of them, and no matter how excellent they were individually, small numbers of any type of airplane did not win wars; it is overwhelming numbers that count.

Originally conceived as a three-seater fighter, the Breguet 691 was redesigned and reengined in the spring of 1938 in the assault-bomber configuration, as a two-seater. In its nose it carried a forward-firing 20-mm Hispano cannon and a pair of 7.5-mm MAC machine guns as well as an internal bomb load. This midwing twin-engine monoplane was progressively developed into the Bre 693 and 695 by 1939.

The low-level ground-attack concept took hold due to the mistaken view that monoplane aircraft of "high performance" with a low drag factor would be unable to dive-bomb. This assumption was proven incorrect over and over again during World War II, but in the late 1930s it was accepted by most major air forces, including the French, hence the Breguet 691 concept. This photo shows French Bre 691 aircraft. They went bravely into battle against the German armored columns in Belgium in May 1940 but were slaughtered wholesale by the waiting enemy flak gunners and achieved nothing. (SHAA, Paris)

The French army ordered 125 of the attack model in 1938 and the first joined their units in October the following year. In all, 275 were built and 140 were accepted into service, but there were only 45 actually fit for combat service by April 1940. Although designed as a low-level "hedge-hopping" aircraft, the Breguet was capable of shallow dive-bombing at a 45-degree angle from a height of 3,000 feet. Rather than taking advantage of a built-in capability, the Breguet pilots dive-bombed because of combat conditions. French General Maurice Gamelin complained bitterly in his memoirs how he and like-minded officers had favored dive-bombers but that the Armée de l'Air as a whole opposed them on technical grounds.

The French navy eventually got government permission to order its own home-built Loire-Nieuport LN 411 single-seater dive-bombers designed for antisubmarine work from carriers. In the interim it placed orders for the Vought V-156F two-seater dive-bomber with a US company. Neither aircraft was perfect for the job, but both were eventually to serve in a bloody combat ashore, hence their inclusion here. Both were monoplanes with retractable undercarriages but neither had much in the way of punch in either guns or bomb capacity. Nor, of course, were the naval air crews trained to work with troops—such an eventuality would have seemed inconceivable in 1939.

In the Far East it was Japan that had initiated the wars of conquest against Manchuria, then China proper, and finally received a couple of sharp lessons from the Russians. It therefore had the longest period of actual combat conditions against a large opposing army in which to work out the best methods and develop specialized aircraft. The Japanese navy flew dive-bomber missions from carriers in direct support of the army and marines while incidents were confined to the coast, but

A Japanese army dive-bomber over China. The sturdy, stubby shape of the Mitsubishi Ki-51 ground-attack developed from the Ki-30 light bomber. Designed specifically to operate from airfields close to the front line in the rugged terrain of mainland China during the Sino-Japanese conflicts of the 1930s, the "Sonia" (as it was later dubbed by the Allies), proved very dependable. Some 1,459 were built as Type 99 between 1940 and 1944, and it saw considerable service in other Pacific war zones. (Author's collection, courtesy of Koku-Fan)

thereafter handed over such work to its long-range shore-based bombers, which flew from Formosa. As a result, the Japanese navy was conducting the strategical bombing that all other major air forces were preaching, while the Japanese army felt the need for more and more short-range tactical bombers working from the front line using primitive air strips.

It is the Japanese army aircraft types that most concern us here. Initially the type most used were the *keibaku* (light bomber), and these were organized in groups (*sentais*). Typical of the equipment employed was the Kawasaki Ki-32 ("Mary"), a two-seat, single-engine, low-wing monoplane with a fixed undercarriage. It entered service with the Japanese forces fighting in China during 1938 and proved adaptable and popular with its crews. It was a bomber, not a strafer, and mounted only a single fixed forward-firing 7.7-mm type 89 machine gun over the engine and carried less than 1,000 pounds of bombs. Very similar in design, armament, and performance was the contemporary Mitsubishi Ki-30 ("Ann"), which also entered service with the troops in China in 1938.

From combat experience with these two types of aircraft, Captain Yuzo Fuijita saw the need for a more specialized machine directly able to support the army by ground attack close to the front line. The Japanese army issued a specification that was taken up by the Mitsubishi

40

Company which eventually produced the Ki-51 assault plane (codenamed "Sonia"). This aircraft proved most successful on its introduction into service in 1940. It was again a single-engine, two-seat, low-wing monoplane. It featured a fixed undercarriage and was armed with two wing-mounted 7.7-mm machine guns and could carry a 441-pound bomb. It was highly maneuverable and was protected with 6-mm steel armor plates beneath its engine and cockpit. So well did it perform in the close-support role that it continued to serve throughout the war and a fresh production line was set up for it as late as 1944. Like its near contemporaries the German Junkers Ju 87 and, in different context, the British Fairey Swordfish, the slow and small Mitsubishi Ki-51 carried out its role perfectly. All three machines were derided by their opponents, but all three delivered the goods exactly as required of them, and all went on to exceed the combat life of most of their "far superior" successors. They proved that speed, the one and only criterion by which Western air critics seem to judge warplanes, was not always the most important consideration.

Only the Soviet Union remained consistent during this decade of advance. Their well-established Polikarpov R-5 and SSS squadrons continued to perfect the low-level approach, but the need for a modern replacement was clearly seen by the army leaders. Unfortunately, in Stalin's purge of the officer class any doctrines or ideas associated with the executed "plotters" were tainted by mere association.

Despite this self-inflicted handicap, a remarkable pair of aircraft were specially designed for army support, both in low-level and in dive-bombing. They were to reach combat readiness during the approaching world war. The Polikarpov R-10 was a stopgap aircraft which appeared at this time, a two-seat monoplane attack aircraft. But its bomb load was small and the number of forward-firing guns was only two. It was similar to American attack planes of the same vintage; indeed the Soviets purchased a pair of Vultee V-11Gs that had been passed over in the United States for the A-17.

It was in 1938 that really significant changes were initiated. This year saw the introduction of the rocket projectile into service as a ground-attack weapon. It was previously used mainly as an air-to-air weapon of little accuracy, but the Soviets saw the power of such a device if used from the air against ground targets. Their RS-132 air-to-ground rocket made its debut as early as 1939. Among the new aircraft brought into service at this time, the late 1930s, was the Sukhoi Su-2. Again a low-wing, single-engine monoplane, it had four wing-mounted 7.62-mm ShKAS machine guns and could carry 1,300 pounds of bombs. Equally important was the fact that its two-man crew was protected against return ground fire by plates of 9-mm armor. These planes were later converted to carry the newly developed RBS-82 ground-attack rockets, and the number of forward-firing machine guns was increased to six.

The Su-2 introduced what was to be the centerpiece of Soviet close-support aircraft for the 1940s, the armored assault plane (*bronirovanny shturmovik*), which the Western press soon abbreviated to Shturmovik in the same manner as they had turned the German *Sturtzkampfflugzeug* into the more digestible (and later famous) Stuka. It was designed with one concept in mind: low-level rocket and strafing attacks on enemy troop positions and concentrations in the teeth of fierce antiaircraft fire. The concept was worked on throughout the last years of peace and the Soviet designer Sergei Ilyushin eventually came up with a single-seat, single-engine, low-wing monoplane. It was armed initially with two wing-mounted 7.62-mm ShKAS machine guns, but already the Soviets were looking ahead to much more worthwhile firepower; two 20-mm ShVAK cannon were also finally carried, which gave it an unbeatable fixed firepower. Either rockets or bombs could supplement this awesome hitting power. Later versions were two-seaters, and the crew could deliver this ordnance onto enemy troops while protected from their wrath by armor plates of between 7- and 12-mm thickness. These plates protected the engine, crew compartment, and fuel tanks of the aircraft. It was really a flying armored box with only the wings and rear fuselage unprotected.

After being impressed by the German dive-bombers in Spain, the Soviet Union put greater efforts into this arm of its tactical air armory. A few experimental types had already been produced, but starting from scratch, the brilliant design team under Vladimir Petlyakov converted a high-altitude, twin-engine monoplane concept into an outstanding dive-bomber, the Pe-2. This aircraft first appeared in 1940 and was a three-seater that could fly as fast as the latest German fighter aircraft. It had two nose-mounted 7.72-mm ShKAS machine guns, internal and external bomb stowage, and dive brakes.

Both these designs serve to show just how far the Soviet Union led the world in the excellent design and application of close-support aircraft at the beginning of the 1940s. The Soviets had also been dedicated to the theory and tactics of the concept for two decades and were fully ready for such warfare. Only an initial shortage of airplanes restricted them.

Let us now examine the various "shooting wars" in which many of these nations' aircraft were evaluated and national theories of close air support were put to the test and improved upon. Great Britain, France, and the United States were notably absent from such detailed and valu-

Soviet close air support, 1930s style. Po-2s and light tanks exercise on the steppe before Stalin's purges of his army turned the clock back and retarded further progress in this direction. (Author's collection)

able combat experience, although all had observers and air attachés sending back reports.

In China the Chinese air force was largely equipped with foreign aircraft, with the German-built He 66CH biplane dive-bombers and the similar Curtiss BF2C "Hawk" employed in the same role. They also had their modern American attack aircraft supplied by Curtiss, Northrop, and Vultee. All these they duly employed against Japanese troop concentrations, initially at Shanghai and then, as they withdrew into the interior, as flying rear guards. No great lessons were drawn from their work for three reasons. First, they were so few in total numbers that they achieved little. Second, the Chinese air crew, although valiant, were not considered to be on a par with their Western counterparts (nor were the Japanese, a widespread myth that was soon to bring humiliating disillusionment to both Britain and the United States). Third, they flew in the face of overwhelming Japanese fighter opposition and took such heavy losses that they soon ceased to have anything but minor irritant value to the enemy.

If little new could be learned from studying the Chinese methods, what of the Japanese? They employed the navy Aichi D1A1 and D1A2 "Susie" biplane dive-bomber, which had been modeled on the German He 66, while operations were still within range of the Japanese aircraft carriers *Ryijo* and *Kaga* off the Chinese coast from July to September 1937. In a British Air Ministry Intelligence memorandum the observer informed a disinterested London that, with regard to the employment of aircraft to support the army:

> The Japanese evidently consider this method of employment to be useful and effective. Level bombing from medium or low altitudes, dive bombing and low flying tactics with light bombs and machine guns are the normal practice. Aircraft are frequently used as an adjunct to artillery in the bombardment of enemy strong points or artillery positions. Dive bombing is carried out by light bombers and fighters and is particularly favoured when no anti-aircraft resistance is expected.[9]

Dive-bombers of the 2d Combined Air Flotilla were utilized in the face of stiff fighter opposition as well during the Japanese attack on the Chinese capital of Nanking in September 1937. When the improved Aichi D3A1 appeared in September 1940, they too were "blooded" in China with the 12th Air Corps. The Aichi "Val" was a single-engine, two-seat, low-wing, monoplane dive-bomber again with a fixed under-carriage with spatted wheels like the Stuka. It could carry a single 550-pound bomb under the fuselage and two smaller bombs under the wings, and there were also two forward-firing 7.7-mm type 97 machine guns. Improved into the D3A2, the Val was to become the Stuka of the Pacific with a long and highly successful career against shipping targets. But as a ground-support aircraft the earlier models of the Val continued to cut their teeth against targets deep in the heart of the Chinese mainland. The 14th Air Corps equipped with this machine moved into Vichy French airfields in Indochina in the autumn of 1940 and from here they struck at hitherto "safe" Chinese airfields, hitting Kunming on 7 October.

Perhaps the Chinese offered no great challenge, but the Japanese also took lessons from two bloody incidents in which they clashed with the Soviet Union in this period. The standard Soviet light bomber was the Tupolov SB-2 (*skorostnoi bombardirovshchik* or high-speed bomber), which also fought with the Chinese and Spanish Republican forces. It was a twin-engine, mid-wing monoplane, a light bomber of the conventional type. The first clash took place at Lake Khasan in July 1938 and 150 of these aircraft flew against Japanese positions unopposed. By the time of the much more serious Khalkin River incident on the Mongolian/Manchukuo border in May 1939, the Japanese had five hundred of their own aircraft ready to fight back.

The climax of the rapidly escalating air battles came when the major Soviet land offensive was unleashed by General Grigori Zhukov. A Soviet Independent Armored Brigade was sent in behind the Japanese defenders at Khalkin Gol on 20 August 1939. The Russian tank columns were well supported by no less than two hundred bombers. The SB-2 flew with the 32d, 38th, and 150th Bomber Regiments. These regiments went into action against ground targets in waves of up to sixty machines at a time with heavy fighter cover in the manner conceived by the now purged Tukhachevsky. The Japanese again came out the loser in this brief encounter but set about organizing their own close-support needs in readiness for the next.

The Italian operations in Ethiopia were not significant because the opposition was merely bands of ill-equipped natives making desperate stands wherever their mountainous terrain offered a chance to hold the advancing columns. But air power was instrumental in both bypassing such blocks and smashing them whenever necessary. The Abyssinians had few fighters with which to oppose the Italian invaders, so any available aircraft could bomb and strafe at will.

One important lesson that was learned from the Italian Ethiopian campaign, however, should not be lightly dismissed even though it cannot be considered direct support. This was the use of transport aircraft in large numbers to influence the war on the ground. The rapid movement of troops was later emphasized by the acclaimed work of twenty Junkers Ju 52s in transporting 1,500 Moroccan troops to reinforce General Francisco Franco's insurgents at the start of the Spanish Civil War. Transport aircraft were used not only to airlift vital troop reinforcements to where they were needed quickly, but also to fly in essential fuel and supplies, without which the most powerful tanks and motorized troop columns would soon have ground to a halt. The new blitzkrieg tactics then taking shape in Russia and Germany depended on speed and mobility for their success.

Tanks are thirsty vehicles, and once out of fuel they change from unstoppable juggernauts to inert and almost helpless heaps of junk. The Germans operated fleets of old Junkers Ju 52 three-engine transports which were looked on with scorn by their opponents. Their value was that they kept the front-line Stuka dive-bomber bases quickly supplied with bombs and fuel by airlifts. The close-support aircraft could therefore move their bases almost daily to keep up with the advance on land without having to rely on land transport, which was disrupted, slow, and vulnerable. The Ju 52s also dropped paratroops to seize vital bridges and take forts to aid the army. So they were almost as much a part of the close-support scene as were the dive-bombers, the strafing fighter, or the

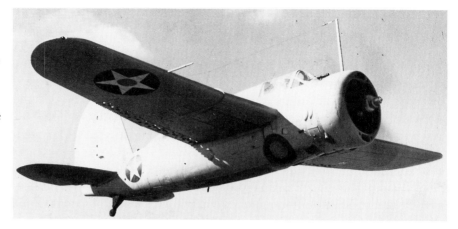

Not all ideas realized their potential. Here is a US Navy SBN-1 adapted from a Brewster dive-bomber design. Although it promised much when first unveiled in 1936, subsequent planes developed from it proved lacking despite many orders, notably from the US Army, the RAF (as the Buccaneer) and the Dutch air force in 1940. The final fate of this much modified series of aircraft was as a target tug and not an attack bomber. (US National Archives, Washington, DC)

Panzer. The British, French, Americans, and even the Soviets had no such aerial workhorse organization with which to keep their front-line aircraft in play in a similar fast-moving scenario.

The final rehearsal for World War II was the Spanish Civil War. The Germans and the Italians intervened on behalf of the Nationalist and Falangist forces under General Franco, the Soviet Union on behalf of the Republicans, a raggle-taggle group of varying shades of the political spectrum from conservatives to anarchist, but which became increasingly dominated by the more single-minded Communists. The two Western democracies wrung their hands and preached nonintervention when it was obvious from the start that nobody but them was practicing it.

The war was fought in the old-fashioned way but with modern concepts overlayed. Thus, slow-moving columns of troops marched on dug-in established lines of defense around crucial cities. But gradually the influence of both the ground-attack aircraft and the tank made victory for Franco inevitable despite heroic sacrifice and much bloodshed. Atrocities and massacres were widely carried out by both sides, but were reported in the press mostly if committed by the Right.

Perhaps the most notorious Spanish Civil War battle involving air power was Guernica. It foreshadowed in minute if hideous detail the differing concepts of how World War II air power was to be used—the scalpel of the dive-bomber or the steamroller of the heavy bomber. At Guernica it was the latter that "won" the day when the same military objective could have been obtained far more accurately and easily, and with no loss of civilian life, by the employment of dive-bombers. Thus it preceded the difference between the German operations at Sedan in 1940 and the German bombing of Rotterdam or London or the even more devastating British firestorms of Hamburg and Dresden. Tactical or Strategical? Precision or terror?

Luftwaffe close-support involvement crystallized during its intervention with the Legion Kondor from November 1936 onward. The original commander, General Hugo Sperrle, was replaced by General Wolfram Freiherr von Richthofen in November 1938. Von Richthofen's name was to become synonymous with the blitzkrieg in World War II, but in 1936, as Sperrle's chief of staff, he was learning like everyone else. The Stuka made its debut on the Ebro front in conjunction with land attacks by General Ritter von Thoma. It won instant acclaim. Luftwaffe officers in Spain claimed that it could drop its load within five meters of a target. In the subsequent Aragon campaign, the Luftwaffe were very concerned that the enemy might capture one intact (even Nationalist pilots were not allowed to examine them).[10]

Around this time, September 1936, the first of the new generation of dive-bombers, the Junkers Ju 87A-1, were being evaluated at the Rugen center. Three of these machines were being used by Bomber Group K/88. The Junkers Ju 87 was a two-seat, single-engine, inverted gull-wing monoplane with a fixed undercarriage. The Junkers Ju 87 carried a single 1,000-pound bomb in a swinging crutch under its fuselage and had fixed forward-firing MG17 machine guns in the wings. It had dive brakes and an automatic pull-out device and was designed to dive-bomb and nothing else. One test pilot who flew all types of aircraft described it as the perfect machine for the job—it felt right once you stood it on its nose. The Junkers Ju 87 became known merely as the "Stuka" and was in turn feared and dreaded, debunked and derided,

It was the Junkers Ju 87 "Stuka" that epitomized close air support during the first three years of the war. Although a slow aircraft, it was extremely strong and highly maneuverable. Its loss rate was among the lowest of all bombing aircraft despite often repeated claims of vulnerability, but even had its rate been the highest the Stuka would have been more than justified by the results it achieved. Poland, Norway, Belgium, France, Yugoslavia, Greece, and Crete, as well as large parts of the Soviet Union and North Africa, all felt the precision power of the Stuka. Here a Staffel peels off to land at its forward base in southern Russia after another successful support mission. (Author's collection)

scorned and envied, depending which end you were on once it commenced its vertical attack dive. Fitted with wind-driven sirens to enhance the natural scream of a descending aircraft (the so-called "Trombones of Jericho") to further destroy enemy morale, its accuracy was phenomenal. Although it was slow and poorly defended, it could linger over the battlefield, it could hit what it aimed at, it was rugged and strong so it could operate from anywhere close behind advancing troops, and it worked! Love it or hate it, the Stuka was perhaps the most effective and famous close-support aircraft of all time.[11]

This has a certain irony, for the man most associated with it, von Richthofen, was initially far from enamored of the plane and was more interested in the low-level strafers like the Hs 123. In Spain, however, the Stuka found its potency. At first three of the original Ju 87A-1s were sent out, but in 1938 they were replaced by three of the modified Bs with spatted instead of trousered undercarriages and improved engine and armaments. Air crews were rotated so that many got their chance to fly close-support as well as back-area interdiction missions against targets like transports and road bridges.

It was just such a mission, to cut off a garrison from its supply route by knocking out a 75-by-25-foot road bridge leading to the little town of Guernica, that occupied von Richthofen's attention in Spain. To achieve its destruction the Germans committed no less than forty-three aircraft, fighters and level bombers, based at Burgos and Vitoria airstrips. It was a sledgehammer to crack a nut indeed. But was all this force necessary? Not if the dive-bombers had been employed.

> . . . He had at his disposal a weapon far more suited to the task than the cumbersome Junkers (Ju 52). Each of his Stuka dive bombers was capable of carrying a single bomb weighing 1,000 pounds. Equipped with the latest bombsight, able to nose-dive onto a target, any of the four Stukas available that day would have had a high chance of taking out the bridge with one direct hit. Even a near miss with such a bomb would have set up a powerful shockwave that, if it did not cause the bridge to collapse, would doubtless have made it unsafe for traffic.[12]

According to one historian, Lieutenant Hans Asmus, "Von Richthofen never considered using the Stukas."[13] Von Richthofen was not to make the mistake of not using dive-bombers again. In World War II he was to be in command of Fliegerkorps VIII, which became *the* exponent of this form of attack in close-support operations.

four

Schwerpunkt!

In Germany the Luftwaffe's commitment to close air support was total. It had been the amazing effect of even a modest scale of low-level attack in Spain that impressed many, including Lieutenant-Colonel Wolfram Freiherr von Richthofen himself. In March 1937, during the Spanish Civil War, three Heinkel He 51 fighters, each carrying six 10-kilogram bombs, were sent in against fortified Republican positions on the northern front. The results were successful beyond the Germans' best expectations and made a great impression on friend and foe alike. Further attacks were made, with the He 51s flying up to seven sorties a day. Nine-plane formations swooped down to 500 feet to release their missiles, and the defenders fled.

As a consequence, three whole squadrons of He 51s were organized by von Richthofen into *Schlacht* (ground-attack) units, and he also began experimenting with direct radio communication from the ground for control of the attacking planes. As we have seen, when the Germans began to use Hs 123s and Ju 87s in the Luftwaffe the close-support scenario was almost complete. At first there was strong opposition to the close-support idea from the more conventional air chiefs, but the attractiveness of paralyzing an enemy army with local air supremacy would prove irresistible.

The quintessence of the close air support ideology was embodied in the German Air Field Manual No. 16 which specified that *all* available aircraft were to be committed to force a decision at a vital point—the *Schwerpunkt* concept. Although the Germans realized that specialized machines and dedicated mission training were prime requirements, there was to be no hesitation in throwing in every aircraft they had to achieve a breakthrough by the land forces:

> The methods of cooperation with army forces will vary in accordance with the current situation, the time factor, the nature of the mission, the objectives in mind, factors of terrain, and the strength and nature of the forces available. No fixed pattern exists. The prime requirement is that the mission must produce results of decisive importance for the army.
>
> For the bomber forces it is thus important to attack those targets whose neutralization will best serve the interests of the army forces or give them the best support in executing their missions, or which will achieve most in thwarting the plans of the enemy.
>
> The more closely the opposing armies are locked in battle, and the closer the decisive moment approaches, the greater will be the effectiveness of action by the bomber forces in and near the front-line areas.[1]

This concentration of the maximum available effort on one point before moving on to the next task meant a stage-by-stage methodical demolition of every obstacle to the rapid advance of the land force and was ideal for the continental type of wars that Hitler and his military chiefs intended to conduct.

An important contributing factor in applying the Schwerpunkt was up-to-date knowledge of the enemy dispositions. The time lag between asking for an air strike and its delivery was as crucial a factor in its success as the accuracy with which it was delivered. Thus a good signaling system was essential, and the Luftwaffe were early into this field. The German signal teams were an integral part of the Luftwaffe organization, as were the antiaircraft (flak) gunners. This integration of all arms also gave the Germans a sharp edge over the slow, disorganized fumblings of the Polish, British, and French air forces they were to fight. Each signals regiment would have signal companies equipped with radio, telephone, wireless telegraphy, and teleprinter networks linking the attack squadrons via a central control. They even had Ju 52 transports fitted out as flying communications centers which could be switched to follow the ebb and flow of fast-moving battles. Concentration of the Stuka and Hs 123 forces close to the main assault areas was the prime consideration.

Although the Luftwaffe developed specialized aircraft to a previously unheard-of degree in World War II, it was their ready adoption of the total concept of close air support as a viable and cost-efficient way of waging war that ensured their early, easy mastery in this field. Thus they readily committed all types of bombing aircraft to support land breakthroughs. This was known as the *Schwerpunkt* concept whereby concentration of strength could force a vital point and lead to the envelopment of superior enemy forces. Here a twin-engine Junkers Ju 88-A4 bomber is being readied on its forward airfield for such a mission. (Franz Selinger)

The need was for the Luftwaffe and army headquarters to be in close proximity to each other. Planning called for the identification of specific targets to be hit from the air in a massed assault as the ground forces moved off. These targets were either allocated by army intelligence (existing fortresses or prepared lines of defense, dug-in artillery, or trench works) or located by the vast numbers of reconnaissance airplanes deployed by the Germans. These latter would be able to use photo reconnaissance to pick out specific targets like massing tank formations, concentrating cavalry, infantry divisions detraining at railheads close behind the front line, and so on.

Exact timing was called for so that the survivors of a Stuka attack, still stunned by the blast and concussion of the bombs, or with their heads still well down listening for the whine and howl of the dive-bombers' sirens, would be caught by the advancing German soldiers before they could recover. Keeping the enemy off balance and disoriented was as important as wiping him out by direct hits. Once fear and panic were instilled in a unit it took time to steady it, and the Germans were able to exploit that time by using fast-moving forces to penetrate and surround the enemy, thus creating yet more uncertainty. By not allowing the enemy time to think, to act, to form a firm line, and by slamming him from the air whenever any signs of a stand were observed, a reeling punch-drunk opponent could be turned into a fleeing and defeated one within a short while.

As the attacking German forces moved forward, the opposing air components were disorganized. Not accustomed to fast moves and chained to static bases with concrete and tarmac runways, oil pipelines, and the like, the Germans' opponents could not cope. The Polish, Belgian, Dutch, and French airfields were quickly overrun, their ground crews dispersed, their armament and fuel supplies destroyed or captured. Conversely, the German Stukas had been designed as rugged machines able to operate from the most primitive of improvised airstrips. That ugly fixed undercarriage might slow it down, but the Junkers Ju 87 could land on the rutted, muddy fields of Poland and Flanders, where it would be rebombed and refueled by mobile bowsers brought in by way of immediately established radio and telephonic communication with their last base, and be ready to fly again within a short period. Each Stuka wing or group would be connected to both the main headquarters and the mobile forward control posts advancing with the tanks. Map grid references sufficed as target locators except for fixed targets to be hit, like bridges and rail stations, which were already plotted.

Even the RAF was forced to admit later that

> . . . the Luftwaffe, in applying tactical bombing power in co-operation with the Army, supported it whole-heartedly, and as a matter of deliberate policy was prepared to throw in its long-range bomber force for strategic operations intended to aid the Army in decisive engagements. The conception of co-operation with the Army was as generous as it was efficient in details of aircraft recognition and wireless signals in the field. There was promptness in bombing, and accuracy, intensiveness, and effectiveness in the execution of operations.[2]

In essence, then, the Luftwaffe on the outbreak of war was the exact opposite of the RAF in every vital respect concerning close air support. The most important element was flexibility. If the German long-range bombers were to be thrown into land battles when required, so, in the same generous interpretation of "support," were the short-range dive-bombers quickly switched from immediate front-line duties to the back areas of the enemy forces. In these German interdiction missions, the dive-bombers were used to destroy vital bridge links, rail communications, ammunition dumps, oil supplies, and road transport, and also to deliberately create panic in rear-area infantry concentrations.

The basic Stuka formation was the *Kette* (flight) of three aircraft, three of which, or nine machines, formed a *Staffel* (squadron). In turn three *Staffeln* formed a *Gruppe* with the addition of a *Stab* (staff) flight. In turn three groups, each group of thirty aircraft, were combined into a *Geschwader* (wing). Finally there were *Luftflotten* (air fleets) whose composition varied enormously according to the conditions on the fronts they were working. *Fliegerkorps* (air corps) within individual fleets could also vary according to campaign requirements. Von Richthofen's Fliegerkorps VIII became the most famous, and eventually the main specialist ground-support unit of the Luftwaffe during the Polish, French, Balkan, and Russian campaigns and was always in the spearhead of these outstandingly successful blitzkrieg operations.

The first nation to feel the "benefits" of this enthusiasm and dedicated application were the Poles when World War II began on 1 September 1939. In preparation for this onslaught on Poland, ten Stukagruppen and the solitary remaining Schlachtgruppe, still equipped with the Henschel HS 123 biplane, were all concentrated on forward airfields and their initial tasks were almost all back-area attacks designed to destroy the Polish air force on the ground.

Under Luftflotte I were IV(Stuka)/LG 1, I/St.G 1, II and III/St.G 51, and the special naval unit, 4 (Stuka)/186. Under Luftflotte 3 was III/St.G 51 and under Luftflotte 4 was I/St.G 76, Stab, I and II/St.G 77, and I/St.G 2. II(Schlacht)/LG 2 was based at Alt Rosenburg.

In the beginning of the war there were only a few specialized strikes in more direct support of the troops, such as Bruno Dilley leading a Kette from St.G.1 in a pinpoint attack, launched fifteen minutes before zero hour, to prevent vital bridges being blown by the Poles. In fact, bad weather aborted most of these plans and attacks did not go in until later in the day.

Despite this, as early as Day 1 the Stukas were dictating events in the land battles. I/St.G 2 and I/St.G 77 located and decimated a mixed Polish infantry and transport column near Wielun and I/St.G 76 bombed troops dug in around Lublinitz.

What of the Polish riposte to the German attack? There were twelve squadrons of P-43 Karas, with a strength of 210 machines, available on 1 September. The British Air Ministry claimed that:

> By the end of the first day [1 September 1939] large numbers
> of Polish aircraft were already destroyed on the ground and the

greatest (and most important part) of the ground organisation was very seriously damaged. On the second day, Luftwaffe operations were renewed from the early morning, with the most important airfields as well as a large number of fresh ones again as the objective. Such success was gained that by the end of this day superiority was complete. The Polish aircraft that remained intact had dispersed to small isolated landing grounds with no communications and hence no possibility of co-ordinated operations.[3]

The truth with regard to the Polish Karas was that only three of these machines were destroyed on the ground during the first two weeks of fighting because the Poles had very wisely dispersed their aircraft to secret locations before 1 September. This preserved the aircraft, but unfortunately a change in policy the year before caused the planes to be squandered rather than used in concentrated attacks against the German spearheads. No less than five squadrons were subordinated to various Polish armies on mainly reconnaissance duties.

This left only a few of the Kara squadrons available for the attack role with the Bomber Brigade. These aircraft were secretly moved to forward combat airfields between 27 and 31 August. They were in action from the second day of the German attack but took heavy losses from the mobile flak units which accompanied the enemy columns. An assault by eighteen Karas of 64 and 65 Squadrons was pushed home but resulted in the loss of seven machines and severe damage to three more. The next day twenty-five Karas from 21, 22, and 55 Squadrons hit German armor near Radomsko and claimed to have damaged a large number of tanks. Further attacks were made in the following week against German tanks advancing on the central front as well as to the north around Pultusk. Again successes were claimed, but the German columns were not halted and the number of Karas rapidly dwindled to a handful which could do nothing to stem the tide. With the Polish defenses now completely overwhelmed, German attacks finally did catch the bulk of the remaining aircraft on the ground, and nineteen were destroyed.

After 3 September the Luftwaffe could devote its entire strength to fully cooperating with the Panzers in the encirclement and total destruction of the various Polish armies in the field. The Hs 123s were also extremely active, flying as many as ten sorties a day from makeshift fields that changed from day to day. Equally committed in the strafing role with their 20-mm cannon and machine guns were the Me 110 twin-engine fighters of I/LG 1.

General A. Armengaud of the French air force gave this eyewitness account of German close-support methods in a report he later delivered to a complaisant general headquarters:

> The German system consists essentially of making a breach in the front with armor and aircraft, then to throw mechanised and motorized columns into the breach, to beat down its shoulders to right and left in order to keep on enlarging it, at the same time as armored detachments, guided, protected and reinforced by aircraft, advance in front of the supporting divisions in such a way that the defense's maneuverability is reduced to impotence. It would be madness not to draw an exact lesson from this pattern and not to pay heed to this warning.[4]

Wasted words! Meanwhile the Stukas now dominated the Polish battlefields, roaming hither and thither and smashing Polish cavalry units, troop trains, railway junctions and stations, and vital bridges. Even the RAF had to give grudging acceptance to this fact: "The outstanding success of the campaign was the successful use of the JU 87 dive bomber. With little or no opposition to hamper them the units equipped with this aircraft were able to exploit the accuracy of bomb aiming inherent in the steep dive, as well as the demoralising effect on personnel exposed to dive-bombing attacks."[5]

Perhaps the greatest of their many achievements was their role in smashing the only serious Polish counterattack when twelve divisions of their Army of Posen, under General Kutrzeba, tried to move against the flanks of the German 8th and 10th Armies advancing on Warsaw north of the Pilica River. Launching his divisions south across the Bzura River on the night of 9–10 September, he penetrated the screening infantry. The situation looked grim for the Germans with both their armies outflanked, and an urgent appeal went out for all available aircraft to plug the gap.

The Hs 123s of II/LG 2 under Captain Weiss were sent in to conduct low-level attacks on the heads of the Polish columns at Bielawy and Piatek. This they did, scattering the enemy with both their bombs and the mere noise of their engines at full revs just above the soldiers' heads. More substantial help came in the forms of the Stukas, now based at various forward strips around Radom. They attacked all the enemy columns seen in the Kutno region, inflicting crippling losses. Equally important, they cut the bridges over the Bzura, thus cutting off the Polish advance guard from the reserves.

The Polish commander General Kutrzeba later recorded what it was like to be on the receiving end of the Stukas in full cry: "Towards ten o'clock a furious air assault was made on the river crossings near Witkovice—which for the number of aircraft engaged, the violence of their attack, and the acrobatic daring of their pilots, must have been unprecedented. Every moment, every troop concentration, every line of advance came under pulverizing bombardment from the air. It was just hell on earth. The bridges were destroyed, the fords blocked, the waiting columns of men decimated."[6]

By 12 September the Poles were largely beaten in the field and dive-bomber units were recalled to Germany. Only the mopping-up of fortresses at Warsaw and Modlin remained. The three-week campaign had cost the German army just 8,000 dead, 218 tanks, and 31 Stukas.

The system had worked so perfectly that it required only some fine-tuning before it was applied to the western front. However, stalling by the German commanders and bad weather gave the Allies an eight-month breathing space in which to absorb the fate of Poland and prepare themselves. "Hitler has missed the bus!" chortled British Prime Minister Neville Chamberlain the day before Germany invaded both Denmark and Norway. The former surrendered without resistance but Norway required a couple of weeks to subdue as British and French troops were hastily flung ashore at central and northern ports to assist. Little new in the way of ground support was required to overcome this defense. Just one Luftflotte sufficed with only a single Stukagruppe. The Stukas divided their missions between blasting the road blocks on the road north and attacking the Allied fleets. This was enough and soon the surviving Allied troops were on their boats going home.

The focus of attention now switched to the south. Belgium, Luxembourg, and the Netherlands clung stubbornly to neutralism despite the examples of their two neighbors. This served only to hamper the British and French from helping them and suited the Germans perfectly. The Germans' finalized plan was to lure the Allied main armies forward into Flanders by methodical attacks on the Benelux nations. The Allied plan was to conform exactly, for the British and French armies relied on anchoring their right flank on the Maginot line and wheeling the main armies northeast.

But the main power of the German attack came from their armored and motorized divisions, under generals Heinz Guderian and Hans Reinhardt, which were to advance via the "impassable" Ardennes forests, cross the Meuse at Montherme and Sedan, and slice across northern France, severing the Allied armies from their main supplies and reserves. This was the *Sichelschnitt* (Sickle Cut) battle plan which later many people claimed to originate. The battle commenced on 10 May 1940 and the results were catastrophic for the western powers and brilliantly success-

ful for the Germans. The German air operations in this battle were the purest examples yet of the close-support system working at its best. Like the Poles before them, the Allied air strikes were weak, ill coordinated, costly, and completely ineffectual.

The Germans had 324 Stukas and 42 Hs 123s mainly under von Richthofen's VIII Fliegerkorps. The long-range bombers were again sent in to wipe out Allied air forces on their runways while the Stukas were assigned the tasks of subduing Belgian forts and defenses around Liege and then supporting the armored breakthrough on the Maas and Meuse rivers.

The Allied air forces were poorly equipped to offer their troops the same backing. As we have seen, the RAF had no close-support aircraft worthy of the name. Ten squadrons of Fairey Battles and ten of Bristol Blenheim light bombers were allocated to the Advance Air Striking Force but they were incapable of attacking moving targets on the spur of the moment as the Stukas could. Even against fixed targets they proved ineffective. The Westland Lysander was nothing more than a reconnaissance

In the late 1930s the RAF put all its light-bomber eggs into one basket, the Fairey Battle three-seater, scorning dive-bombing completely and relying on the shallow approach. As a direct result of this policy, when war came squadron after squadron of these close-support bombers were shot out of the sky by German flak gunners at the Maas and Meuse bridges in May 1940, and the RAF support squadrons were decimated. (RAF Museum, Hendon, London) machine that had little or no attack potential. There was no close-support policy so there were no aircraft for the job.

Nonetheless, attempts were made. At midday on 10 May thirty-two Battles were dispatched against German columns advancing through Luxembourg. They attacked in four waves of eight and despite meeting no fighter opposition, thirteen Battles were destroyed by the German flak and most of the others were damaged. This strike was repeated by the same number of Battles three hours later with the loss of ten more of the British bombers. The next day eight Battles were sent against the same target, seven were shot down, and the last one returned without even reaching the target. The same day nine Battles of the Belgian air force went to attack three bridges over the Albert Canal. They lost six of their number before even reaching the target and the other three did no damage whatsoever. Finally twelve Blenheims were sent against the same target and four were destroyed, the rest damaged, again for no result at all. On and on it went in brave futility. Nine Blenheims were sent off on 12 May to attack German tanks near Tongeren, two returned and the tanks kept rolling. The main British air effort was the attacks on the Maas and Meuse bridges on 14 May when forty of the seventy-one Battles and Blenheims dispatched were shot down. One of the last attempts to prove that British light bombers could influence land battles was made on 17 May when twelve aircraft of 82 Squadron were directed to strike at German tanks near Gembloux, twelve miles north of Namur. Only one returned.

So much for the light bombers of the RAF. What of the French effort? They had a few specialized ground-attack aircraft but not enough. The main units were Groupement 18/GBA with the twenty-four Breguet 693s of I and II/54, some still lacking bomb-release equipment which had to be installed a day after the German assault commenced. Eighteen of these machines struck at German tank columns at Tonges on 12 May, and only ten survived. One of the French aircrew, Sergeant-Gunner Conill, was to recall this attack:

> There was the main road, the one we were looking for, flanked by trees and ditches. And what a sight! Hundreds and hundreds of vehicles rolling towards France, following each other at short intervals and travelling fast. A lovely target! At 350-km an hour, right down the axis of the road, flying at tree top level, the Major attacked. . . . Suddenly white and blue flashes burst out beneath us and there was a hellish outburst of fire and steel and flames, growing more intense. I clearly saw the strings of small-caliber shells, climbing towards us by the thousand.[7]

They lost two machines. This left the group with only twelve serviceable aircraft, eight of which were sent against pontoon bridges on the Meuse and enemy troops at Bazeilles. They repeated the operation the next day with nine, striking at the Montherme crossings. They were by far the most successful of all the Allied attackers and on 31 May GBA 18, with six Breguet 693s, made an attack on German tanks massing on the Channel coast south of Abbeville, losing one of their number in the process.

Both their success and their accuracy stemmed from the fact that they had abandoned the low-level approach and were now conducting dive-bombing, albeit at shallow angles. No less than eighteen aircraft were assembled for one such attack at first light on 5 June against a German armor column attacking south across the river Somme at Amiens toward Paris. They hit the target and took no losses. Three hours later twelve Breguets from GBA 19 made similar attacks against German tanks at Chaulnes. On completion of their dive-bombing runs they turned their attention to a column of motorized troops north of Peronne. By reverting back to strafing attacks with their guns and cannon, they left themselves exposed and were jumped by German fighters, losing five of their number.

A few more attacks were made by the French assault flyers as the French army finally disintegrated but, by the armistice, the Breguets had flown five hundred sorties with the loss of forty-seven aircraft. They might have achieved even more but for the fact that the Breguet plants at Bourges and Villacoublay were overrun, and thus all hope of getting replacement aircraft abruptly ceased. This latter fact provides another point in favor of close air support. Heavy long-range bombers might have damaged these factories in precision attacks, but Stuka-led Panzer columns, by actually occupying the plants themselves, were much more effective in halting production, for good.

The only other close-support aircraft to be used in the brief campaign in France and Flanders were from an unexpected source, the Aeronavale dive-bombers. Because the French air crews of these aircraft were not trained for land operations, not too much could be expected of them. Those French aircraft and air crews that survived the initial German bombing attacks were thrown into battle piecemeal and were destroyed in gallant actions in much the same manner as the Breguets.

The two dozen French Loire-Nieuports equipped units AB 2 and AB 4 and the fifty-two Vought V-156Fs equipped units AB 1 and AB 3. The latter unit was never really in the fight, its entire complement of aircraft being destroyed in their hangars at Boulogne-Alprech on the morning of 10 May. Their first return blows, after they had been hastily

Realizing the perilous state of their own aircraft industry after two decades of neglect, the French reacted to the looming war with Germany by hastily seeking modern ground-attack aircraft. From the United States the French navy bought Vought Vindicator dive-bombers as V-156Fs. They were shipped over in small batches until the outbreak of the war and the embargo halted supplies. Only a few squadrons of the Aeronavale had been equipped with these machines at the time of the blitz and they were thrown in piecemeal as land-attack units rather than being used against naval targets. Those that survived the initial German air strikes were employed against the advancing German tank columns, blasting bridges and convoys until they were all virtually wiped out. (Musée de l'Air, Paris)

reequipped with spare aircraft, were struck on 15 May by nine LN 401s of AB 2 which carried out attacks on a German column at Yerseke on the Dutch island of Walcheren without loss. They repeated the dose in company with nine V156Fs of AB 1 the next day and with ten Voughts and three Loires on 17 May. Other Voughts hit German armor at Flessingue with the loss of one of the French aircraft.

All this was very well done but the relative immunity of the French fliers was not to last much longer. The Loire-Nieuport LN 411 bore a remarkable resemblance to the Stuka, being single-engined and with the same inverted gull wing. It had a retractable undercarriage and was much smaller. Its passing similarity was thought on several occasions to have contributed to its survival when encountering German aircraft en route to and from the target. This was more than made up for by the constant attention Allied antiaircraft gunners gave them. Many French LNs were fired at by their own gunners and two were shot down by them.

The most concentrated attack in support of the army was made by the French flyers on 19 May. Operating from Berck airfield, twenty Loires were sent to strike at German tank columns at Berliamont. Most of their promised fighter escort failed to turn up, so the little dive-bombers attacked down from 6,000 feet to 1,000 feet through heavy flak. This proved one of the very few effective Allied air strikes of the campaign. The German advance was delayed forty-eight hours by this

one dive-bombing sortie, but the cost to the French airmen was ghastly. Of the twenty Loires involved, half were shot down over the target. Of the surviving ten, all were hit and put out of action.

The next call for sacrifice came on 19 May when German tanks were rolling unopposed over the bridge at Origny—St. Benoit. Only three Loires from the two units could fly and they joined with the eleven remaining Voughts of AB 1. Again the fighter escorts, British Hawker Hurricanes, failed to turn up, so the dive-bombers set off for the bridges on their own. The faster V-156Fs soon left the three Loires behind them, but this proved lucky for the Loires. The Voughts were ambushed by German fighters and six of the eleven were destroyed. The bombs of the rest missed the target. The trio of Loires arriving later caught the enemy flak on the hop and two managed to carry out their attacks successfully; the other was shot down over the target.

The two surviving French navy Loire aircraft were sent out alone on 21 May to destroy a bridge over the River Aisne and one of them was shot down by antiaircraft fire. The next day they lost both their bases and their ground crews when the Panzers overran Boulogne airfield. Five Voughts attacked a German tank formation just outside the town and then flew to Cherbourg airfield. On the afternoon of 22 May, these five French aircraft conducted two dive-bombing attacks on Fort de la Creche at Boulogne which was occupied by the enemy. For a brief period they operated from the RAF airfield of Tangmere and on 1 June they flew a mission against the German forces at Furnes. After this, most of the surviving machines were evacuated to the south of France for operations against the Italians, where they lost one of their number to fighter attack by a Polish pilot who, perhaps understandably, mistook the Loires for Stukas.

That was the sum of Allied close-support missions. In total it amounted to little. Bravery and courage counted as naught when set against two decades of inefficient policies, too few aircraft, and indifference in high places. It was to take still more tough lessons from the Luftwaffe before there was any change of heart.

As for the Germans, the battle that crushed France, Belgium, and Holland was virtually a rerun of the Polish campaign. The main Stuka attacks were initiated by St.G 77 and went against French defense works on the west bank of the Meuse near Sedan on the afternoon of 12 May. They lost their longtime and much-loved commander, Colonel Gunter Schwarzkopff—the "Stuka Father"—to flak that day, but their attacks were devastating. After a Dornier attack, St.G 2 took up the assault. Artillery positions, pillboxes, antiaircraft guns, and entrenchments were pounded all afternoon by wave after wave of dive-bombers. In all some two hundred Stukas were employed, backed up by medium bombers and fighters. Here was the Schwerpunkt with a vengeance!

Bryan Perrett wrote:

> The incessant howling of the dive bombers, the scream of their bombs and the endless explosions, accompanied by blinding smoke and the shrieks of the wounded, would have strained the nerves of hard-bitten regulars let alone those of these middle-aged and rather unwilling soldiers who thought only of returning to their families. For the infantry, cowering in trenches and bunkers, it was an ordeal which induced deep shock, but for the artillery in their wider gun-pits it was infinitely worse.[8]

By the same evening the German troops were across the river at two places.

The Hs 123s of II/LG 2 under Captain Otto Weiss also made a name for themselves in this campaign. It was largely by their efforts that a dangerous British tank attack south from Amiens toward Cambrai was broken up and dispersed on 22 May. Massed Stuka assaults broke up a much larger attack near Arras, and the only real threat to the German advance was over before it began.

The importance of the close-support squadrons was obvious. The British Air Ministry later summarized it: "As soon as air reconnaissance or ground combat reports established that any points of resistance were holding up, or were likely to hold up the advance, an extreme concentration of air striking power, with up to nine sorties a day for each aircraft, paralysed the British and French armies to a degree that was a revelation even to the Germans themselves. Thus the legend of the dive bomber grew, and the *Blitzkrieg* became a reality."[9]

All this was not achieved by chance. The Stukas had utilized the eight-month breathing space to improve upon their techniques even if the Allies had squandered the time. The RAF attitude was summed up in a memorandum written on 9 May just before the Stuka and Panzer combination was let loose and the low-level Battles were shot down in scores without achieving a single hit. In answer to a query on whether "the prewar policy of neglecting the dive bomber was not quite sound,"[10] the assistant chief of Air Staff (Training) at the British Air Ministry wrote that study of reports from Norway "only confirm what we have known for years—that dive bombing gives greater accuracy than high-level bombing. Low-level bombing, however, has been proved to be more accurate than dive bombing. The question as to whether the dive is really a requirement for the RAF involves many factors. . . . " He added that to adopt steep dive-bombing by the RAF was a formidable task. "I am therefore reluctant to embark on it until we have enough evidence to show that it will be worthwhile."[11]

Helmut Mahlke explains the various modifications to their strategy the Stuka units carried out in the field:

> Target description by telephone, based on maps, was used. This of course caused quite a lot of delay, which was not acceptable for a quick operation. Beginning in France therefore a special organisation was set up. A Stuka UHF wireless set was mounted in a tank of the Panzer force involved in the main battle. Luftwaffe UHF operators in these tanks participated in the main ground attacks, as close as possible to the commander of the Panzer force. Where this system was in operation the Stuka unit was directed overhead and got exact targeting by wireless. In addition the ground troops would shoot coloured flares near the target.[12]

With the French surrendered and the British locked in their own island, the Stukas were switched to strategical missions in connection with the proposed invasion of England, Operation Sealion. Had the German army got ashore at Kent there is no doubt that the close-support units of the Luftwaffe would have carried out their ground-attacking role against the virtually unarmed and unarmored formations of the British home defenses with speed and efficiency. As they did not land, close-support aviation on both sides of the English Channel ceased.

One new idea that did take root on the German side during this period was that of fitting fighter aircraft with bombs for low-level hit-and-run raids across the Channel, the *Jabo* concept. The twin-engine Messerschmitt Bf 110 was not proving much of a success as a fighter, but with two SC 250 (551-pound) bombs slung under its wings it became a fast, low-level attacker of ships and ground targets across the Channel. A special experimental unit, *Erprobungsgruppe* 210, was set up under the command of Captain Walter Rubensdorffer, with two Staffeln of Bf 110C-4Bs. Later another Staffel of the single-engine Bf 109Es was also adapted to carry either a single 551-pound or four 110-pound SC50 bombs under the fuselage in a similar manner, and the idea soon spread to other units. This return to the fighter-bomber concept was to be widely copied by other nations as time went on, and even the highly successful II/(Schlacht)/LG 2 was moved to Brunswick in order to be converted in the late summer of 1940. However this outfit still retained some of its old Hs 123s and it was with a mixture of both new and old types that it was later moved down to support the Balkan campaigns in April 1941.

The Mediterranean campaigns, although small-scale stuff for the Germans after Poland, France, and what was planned for Russia, were the main fighting fronts for the British. Thus while the Germans consolidated and amply demonstrated still further their close-support techniques, the British slowly and reluctantly fumbled toward the same concept, still without much enthusiasm or dedication.

Even when faced with the seemingly imminent landing of Panzers in southern England and a final last-ditch fight for survival, senior RAF officers refused to change their preconceived prejudices. Thus, when the army requested large numbers of small attack dive-bombers which would work closely with the ground forces and be mass-produced in Canada, they were quickly slapped down. The vice chief of the Air Staff stated that: "If the close support question is raised by the Army, I think we must go straight to the Prime Minister on the question of the fundamental strategical principle."[13]

Lord Beaverbrook, the minister for aircraft production, was forced to order dive-bombers directly from the United States, very much against the wishes of the air marshals. In February 1941 Archibald Sinclair at the Air Ministry prevailed upon the secretary of state for war to drop any further demands for dive-bombers. Instead the RAF was content with how things stood, as a memorandum confirmed: "Lysanders [a slow reconnaissance and observation aircraft] can operate satisfactorily when air superiority is maintained. It appears undesirable therefore to rush, regardless of other commitments, into a general re-equipment of Army Co-Operation Squadrons with [P.40] Tomahawks."[14]

At the same time Air Vice Marshall Slessor was continuing to argue that even if the invasion came, "it would be fatal if we are to have bombers scooting about Kent trying to shoot up individual tanks. It is *not* the job of the Air Force to destroy tanks." He went on, "I do not believe in close support at all,"[15] and his view was still widely held in the RAF.

The only aircraft that took part in the first of the North African campaigns in the autumn and winter of 1940 that could be described in any way as close-support machines were the Fiat CR 32s and new Breda Br65 fighter-bombers of the Italian 50 Stormo Assalto and a flight of ancient Gloster Gauntlet single-engine biplane fighters attached to No. 3 Squadron RAAF. They were fitted with 40-pound bombs on makeshift underwing racks and sent into action as "Britain's Answer to the Stuka." Although this merely underlined the bankruptcy of RAF policy

and thinking, they nonetheless operated with some panache during the initial stages of General Archibald Wavell's successful desert campaign.

The Australian unit equipped with Gloster Gauntlet aircraft was based at Gerawla in Egypt with five aircraft and they first practiced their dive-bombing technique on 26 November with mock attacks during an army cooperation exercise with the Western Desert Force. Thus, as prepared as they were ever going to be, the five machines, the last open-cockpit, single-engine, fighter biplanes to be built for the RAF, were then moved forward to Advanced Landing Ground E 74.

On 9 December all five took off at 1235 to carry out a dive-bombing attack on enemy motor transport located on the escarpment northwest of Sofafi. One aircraft aborted the mission but the remaining four carried out their job, returning to base at 1345. On 11 December Italian troops were reported to be in retreat along a track northwest of Halfway House (which was middistance from Sofafi and Halfaya Pass). Five Gauntlets were sent off at 0620 to dive-bomb them but returned at 0750 having failed to locate the target. At 1105 the same morning four of these machines went out again to dive-bomb enemy troops again reported to be retiring from Sofafi. This time there was no doubting the report for they observed about three hundred troops and two hundred motor vehicles strung out in the vicinity of Halfway House. The quartet subjected the ground troops to both dive-bombing and strafing attacks to good effect and returned to rearm. A second strike was made against the same target between 1400 and 1515.

"The Answer to the Stuka!" The bankruptcy of RAF policy between the wars had left the Commonwealth air forces with no dive-bombers at all. To compensate, fighting against the Italian invasion of Egypt, in the western desert, ancient Gloster Gauntlet Mk II bombers of the Royal Australian Air Force's No. 3 squadron, here shown at their base on Gerawla in November 1940, mounted makeshift dive-bombing sorties against the Italian columns. (Australian War Memorial, Canberra ACT)

The following day saw five Gauntlets airborne at 0815 with the object of dive-bombing a concentration of enemy troops in the vicinity of Halfway. They located the target and carried out dive-bombing attacks, returning to base at 0945. This was their final mission, for the battle was over. Three of the Gauntlets, piloted by Flying Officers Rawlinson, Turnbull, and Davidson, returned to Gerawla on 14 December, followed the next day by the remaining pair, flown by Flight Lieutenant Pelley and Flying Officer Perrin.

In the beginning of January 1941, seventy-nine Stukas of Stab/St.G 3, I/St.G 1, and II/St.G 2 moved down to Sicilian airfields with the triple tasks of closing the central Mediterranean to the British fleet, neutralizing Malta as an effective British base, and supporting General Irwin Rommel and his Afrika Korps in retrieving the situation in North Africa. It is the latter task that interests us here. On 31 January, St.G 3 moved from Sicily to Castel Benito, Sirte, and Arco Philernorum airfields and were joined there in February by I/St.G 1. Under the Fliergerfuehrer Afrika these Stukas began attacks in conjunction with Rommel's moves to block any further British advance westward. Their work commenced on 15 February with strikes at forward British army posts at Marsa Brega. However, the situation in the Balkans forced the Germans to divert their attention for a time.

While Hitler braced himself and his victorious forces for the final settlement with Stalin in the east and left the stubborn British to the night attacks of the long-range bombers and the U-boat blockade, world attention turned to the smaller-scale operations in the Mediterranean. The Italians had strong forces in their North African possession and these were expected to invade Egypt, sweep aside the tiny British military presence in the area, and seize Cairo and the Suez Canal. Had they done so, the British would probably have been put out of the war, but the Italians were at first held and then defeated by the British.

Thus, to their exasperation, the Germans were forced to detach a small armored force to their ally's aid and send some of their dive-bomber units down to the area to support the tanks. They also negotiated a deal to supply Junkers Ju 87s to the Italian air force, after both the Italian-built Breda 88 and the Savoia Marchetti Sm 85 had proved to be flops. Italian fighter pilots were also selected to undergo urgent conversion courses at German *Stukaschules* (Stuka schools).

German plans for the invasion of the USSR depended on keeping things quiet in the Balkans so that the British would not be able to interrupt the flow of Rumanian oil. This desire was upset by Mussolini's fool-hardy invasion of Greece and by an insurrection in Yugoslavia that ousted the government friendly to the Axis. In the spring of 1941 the old

After the failure of most of their own homebuilt products, the Italian air force also adopted the Stuka of their German allies and soon produced their own "Aces." Major Giuseppe Cenni (second from right) achieved fame in his precision attacks against British shipping in the eastern Mediterranean in 1941–42. He was killed in 1943 leading a strafing attack in a Macchi fighter-bomber against the Allied beachhead at Salerno. (Author's collection)

tried-and-true combination of Stuka and Panzer was unleashed against both Yugoslavia and Greece. Again the campaigns lasted only a few weeks, and the two nations were crushed even with the British army helping the latter.

On 26 March orders were given for the rapid redeployment of forces from all over Europe at which the Luftwaffe was so skilled. This involved the transfer of one Stukagruppen from El Machima up to Krainitzi in Rumania at short notice. Two additional dive bomber Gruppen, totaling some 120 Junkers Ju 87Bs, were flown from France into Bulgaria and Rumania where they were within striking distance of Belgrade. The whole of the striking force (Stab, I and III/St.G 2, I/St.G 3, and II [Schlacht]/LG 2 in Bulgaria, Stab/St.G 3 and II/St.G 77 in Wiener Neustadt, Austria, Stab, I and III/St.G 77 in Rumania), had assembled under the operational command of General Richthofen.

The German attack on both Yugoslavia and Greece (where the original Italian invasion had been heavily defeated and thrown back by the Greeks themselves) opened on 6 April and by 27 April Athens had fallen. During this time another dive-bomber Gruppe was moved in from France to give overwhelming superiority to the Panzer thrusts through the mountains; they simply brushed aside the Yugoslav, Greek,

The German Balkans campaign, which overran Yugoslavia and Greece in a matter of weeks in the spring of 1941, relied heavily on close support of the troops on the ground by the Luftwaffe to force the mountain passes and defense lines of the Allies. Here a Stuka pilot pulls up after a precision hit on a Yugoslav antiaircraft position at Dubrovnik. (Author's collection)

and British land forces with contemptuous ease. II (Schlacht)/LG 2 was heavily involved in spearheading the German thrust against Skopje and two days later had crossed the Greek frontier and was soon in action against defensive positions at Servia. St.G 77 and Stab/St.G 3 led the main land attacks by the German 2d Army against Belgrade itself. A contemporary account of their effectiveness was given by the War Office:

The greater part of the Yugoslav army was in the north, and the new Simovitch Government had not had time to do more than dispatch large reinforcements to the south. Tens of thousands of men were marching, carrying packs and rifles, with their baggage in ox-drawn wagons which regulated the pace of the columns. The

German air force caught them like that. The dive bombers swooped out of the sky and the long winding column—150 miles jammed with marching men and beasts crawling at a foot pace—were bombed and strafed and blasted. The German aircraft flew along emptying their machine guns when they had used up their bombs on what must have seemed an almost stationary target. That was the end of the Yugoslav reinforcements which should have held the southern passes from Bulgaria.[16]

Mountain passes, artillery posts, vital crossroads, and motorized transport retreating down the valleys toward the Corinth Canal, all were taken under close attack by the Stukas with little opposition from the air. Athens was taken on 27 April and Stukas helped force the Corinth defense line.

The RAF had sent six bomber squadrons to Greece, but as we have seen, they had no close-support aircraft, only Bristol Blenheim light bombers of 11 and 113 Squadrons which were totally inadequate. It is on record that it took 211 Squadron seventeen days to move up from Menidi to Parmythia airfields, or five times the time taken for the Germans to fly in units from France! The Greeks themselves had army cooperation aircraft, one squadron of German-built Henschel 123s, and one squadron of obsolete French-built Breguet 19s some fifteen years old, as well as the usual Battles and Blenheim light bombers.

They could do little to stop the flood. On 10 and 13 April British Blenheims bombed German tanks and motor transport storming down the Varna valley but such pinpricks were exceptional and most of their sorties were fruitless. Soon their forward air bases, so laboriously reached, were being abandoned.

The capture of Crete from the air also involved intensive close-support work from Stuka and Jabo fighters, although the main weight of their attacks was once more directed against the British fleet offshore. By the end of May it was all over.

The story of air-to-surface combat in the first eighteen months of World War II had been one of unprecedented German victory. An air force dedicated to close air support of its troops had triumphed over a succession of enemies that had ignored this principle. The next phase in the European struggle was a much more evenly matched contest.

five

Attrition and Adjustment

The war machine launched by Hitler against the Soviet Union in June 1941 was much the same weapon that had crushed Poland, France, and the Balkan states in the previous three campaigns. Both German and Western opinion about the Russian armed forces' quality and competence was influenced by the Finnish debacle of 1939–40. In this localized conflict the Russians had taken some heavy casualties against the tiny Finnish army, which led many observers to think the Soviet armed forces were inefficient. This theory was found to be badly in error. Certainly the great air fleets and the Panzer divisions that thundered across the Soviet frontier were initially to sweep all before them in much the same manner as earlier. Certainly too the stupidity of Stalin in ignoring the frequent warnings from British Intelligence of what was coming did much to ensure initial German surprise. But this weakness proved temporary.

Thousands of Soviet aircraft were destroyed on the ground in the first days of fighting, thousands more in futile, disorganized attacks against the war-hardened German soldiers. Huge encirclement battles in the true blitzkrieg style netted millions of Russian prisoners and whole armies surrendered or were bypassed. There seemed to be no stopping the Germans in their drive on Moscow, and most observers expected the Russians to be overrun in a matter of weeks.

The Luftwaffe used the same aircraft as before, again throwing everything into the initial strikes and then concentrating on key points of

the battlefield. Two hundred and ninety Stukas were the spearhead as usual, along with forty Bf 110s of I and II/ZG 26, II/ZG 1, and I/SKG (*Schnellfkampf* or fast bomber) 210 being employed exclusively as fighter-bombers in the ground-attack role. The effect of their 20-mm cannon on enemy tank targets was an indicator of future trends. Luftflotte 2 supporting Army Group Center contained seven Ju 87 B Gruppen and the Bf 109Es and Hs 123s of II(Schlacht)/LG 2.

The tactics employed by the German dive-bombers were basically the same as before but with refinements to make them more efficient. A greater number of UHF teams had been formed from Luftwaffe signals personnel and some pilots. They now operated with the army, traveling up with the tank leaders in their own armored command vehicles and acting as forward air controllers. From experience it was found that the closer they operated to the army commanders, the more efficient they were. It was not just a question of learning the UHF procedures to give precise target locations to the Stukas. The targets had to be communicated in the best manner without errors in a fast-moving battlefield environment. This was why signals personnel proved better at the job than ex-Stuka pilots who did the job only occasionally.

There were never sufficient numbers of these highly specialized teams to accompany every army involved in the vast thousand-mile front, but as the Stukas were switched from one key battle zone to another in a refinement of the Schwerpunkt principle, so the air controllers were similarly switched to those army units at the center of the main

A Soviet ground-attack aircraft, a Rata I-17 fighter converted to a dive-bombing role and captured by the Germans at Prushany during their initial advance in June 1941. (Author's collection, via Sellhorn)

battlefronts. In the field the superiority of Luftwaffe signals equipment over the army network was obvious and was in part due to the self-discipline of the air force experts in conveying vital facts and orders concisely and accurately with a minimum of delays.

This basic lesson of close air support—that its efficiency depended on a combination of the right aircraft for the job, air crew trained for the job, and timely and accurate information from the point of contact—had to be learned over and over again by each of the other combatants during the war and again afterward. Hard lessons of war were soon forgotten or pushed to one side in peacetime and had to be learned afresh—this is human nature. Most of the other major powers eventually followed the same road pioneered by the Germans, but it was the Germans who originally got it right, refined it, and carried it through with proven results. It took them to the very gates of Moscow and Leningrad before they were halted.

Several factors brought the 5th German Panzer victory to an abrupt and unexpected halt. The intervention of Hitler in diverting his armies away from the key target of the capital was the most profound cause; the early onset of the Russian winter, for which the Germans were ill prepared, was a second; the heroic fighting qualities and self-sacrifice of the Russian troops in the field was another. The Soviets had also the priceless assets of unlimited manpower and almost limitless land. They could afford to give up both in unbelievable quantities and still go on fighting. They moved their aircraft and tank factories farther eastward and production steadily increased. But ignorance was a vital ingredient in the German failure. They were surprised by the toughness and the vast numbers of Soviet tanks.

They were equally unprepared to find an enemy air force which, notwithstanding appalling disorganization and poor leadership, was as good as and in some ways superior to their own in the area of close air support. Both the Il-2 Shturmovik and the Pe-2 Peshka types came as very unpleasant surprises to the Germans. But the Soviets also threw into combat every manner of aircraft in the ground-attack role. Those employed initially included the Sukhoi Su-2 light bomber and the semiobsolete Polikarpov I-153 fitted with RS-82 rockets and small bombs. Initially the use of rockets against ground targets proved disappointing, but again it was to be imitated by all other air forces with increasing effectiveness. Even if Soviet tactics were primitive, sheer numbers had an overwhelming effect on the German advance.

The Soviets gave as good as they got in the close-support role. Moreover, time was on their side from December 1941 onward; their production steadily increased, as did their knowledge and tactics. During

1942–43 this was to further increase their already quantitative superiority while at the same time producing experts in their fields who brought a better understanding and application of techniques to their combat usage. Thus Ivan Polbin perfected the dive-bombing skills of the Pe-2s with his *Vertushka* ("Dipping Wheel") concept which, as its name indicated, involved a continual circling of the target to keep the enemy flak off balance before a continual series of 70-degree dive-bombing attacks by all the aircraft involved. The low-level attacks of the Il-2s proved hard for the Germans to counter for they found their hitherto effective light flak shells bouncing off the Shturmovik's armored hide! The Soviets also modified the low-level approach into shallow dive-bombing, which was found to be far more accurate in delivery and effective in lowering the morale of the target. The VYa 23-mm cannon also proved a useful modification to Soviet tank-busting capabilities.

Both Germans and Russians progressively upgraded their heavy cannon from 20-mm to 37-mm and then to 75-mm, which could easily penetrate the thickest tank armor. On the German side the 30-mm MK 101 was fitted under the fuselage of the twin-engine Henschel Hs 129B, almost a direct copy of the Il-2 with heavy armor protection. A special modification of the Junkers Ju 87D Stukas called for the fitting of two BK 37-mm which had superb penetrating power and a high rate of fire. With such a weapon, German aces like Hans-Ulrich Rudel went on to knock out hundreds of Soviet tanks.

Perhaps the most famous of all Soviet ground-attack aircraft of World War II was the Ilyushin Il-2 and Il-10 "Shturmovik." Designed by S. V. Ilyushin in 1938 as an "armored ground-attack" aircraft, this two-seater was progressively developed during the war years and earned itself a formidable reputation. This one is preserved at a Polish museum. (Author's collection, via J. Waligora)

The Luftwaffe was among the first of the world's air forces to adapt its high-performance fighters to the role of ground-attack machines, probably due to the dire situation on the Eastern Front after 1943. Their Jabo (fighter-bomber) units performed very well with a single heavy bomb slung under the fuselage on a rack as featured on this Focke Wulf Fw 190, which also carries long-range drop fuel tanks under the wings. (Archiv Selinger)

The Soviet dive-bomber that dominated the ground-attack scene on the Eastern Front between 1943 and 1945 was the Pe-2, here seen in Polish markings. Converted from a high-level fighter design in 1940, this aircraft (along with the American A-36) proved that dive-bombers could be as accurate and as fast, or faster, as defending fighters. The myth that dive-bombers had to be slow, plodding machines or else would lose their accuracy was thus demolished by the Soviets, although that myth lingers on in innumerable histories of air fighting. (Author's collection, via J. Waligora)

Imported American Bell P-39 Airacobra fighters had a 37-mm cannon firing through the propeller hub and thus were eagerly pressed into service in the ground-attack role by the Russians. The fitting of long-barreled N-37 cannon was to make the new Il-2m3 aircraft the bane of the German Panzers. The Stukas' replacement, the Messerschmitt Me 210, proved a failure, however, and the Junkers had to soldier on. More and more it was replaced by Jabo fighters, of which the superlative Focke-Wulf 190A was the best. First introduced in this role in 1942, it could carry a 550-pound bomb beneath the fuselage.

On the Eastern Front both sides used antipersonnel bombs, of which the German version was the SD-2 4-pound fragmentation bomb. They were carried in clusters, fitted with small retarding wings, and designed specifically for use against masses of troops. They could be adjusted to explode on impact or above the ground for maximum spread. The blast released some three hundred smaller shrapnel particles over a radius of some forty feet. A Bf 109 Jabo could carry ninety-six of these at a time. The Germans also tried out the SG131A Forstersonde antitank weapons, which consisted of six automatically triggered downward-pointing rocket launcher tubes firing at an oblique angle.

In the early defensive days the Russians used their large numbers of Po-2 biplanes as night harassment aircraft to keep up a nonstop flow of explosives over the enemy, and this idea was later to be adopted by the Germans when they went over to the defensive.

As well as improving their equipment, the Russians, with experience, became more skilled pilots. Aces appeared, including, uniquely, many women pilots.

Perhaps the most outstanding and famous of the Soviet women dive-bomber pilots of World War II was Nadiezhda Fedutenko. Many of the female pilots who earned fame in the Pe-2 squadrons between 1941 and 1945 were from the Young Communist ranks who, at the age of eighteen, volunteered for the front. But Fedutenko was already a well-known and famous pilot before she joined the ranks of the dive-bomber crews and was given command of her own squadron.

She was twenty-six years old when war broke out in 1941 and from the very first days of the German-Soviet war she was at the front, although still a civilian pilot. She joined a special aviation group based at Kiev in the Ukraine. Here she was assigned many specialized missions, including delivery of ammunitions, equipment, food, and medical supplies to Soviet troops encircled deep behind German lines. She was also involved in flying out badly wounded soldiers from pockets cut off far behind the front. She saved the lives of 150 Soviet soldiers this way.

Another task Fedutenko undertook (while still technically a civilian) early in the war was the flying out of military intelligence data on enemy movements and dispositions. For these jobs she normally used a P-5 aircraft, flying as low as she dared in this slow machine, without any fighter cover or protective armament. This type of flying depended a great deal on her vast store of knowledge and expertise of the area as well as her natural excellence as a pilot.

On one occasion she flew members of the Soviet General Staff out of an encirclement to safety at Kiev. Later it was necessary to deliver bottles of liquid fuel to the front. The landing ground should have been southwest of Kiev, near Rotmistrovka railway station. Fedutenko duly landed her aircraft at the appropriate spot, which she knew perfectly well, without difficulty. However, as the plane touched down and finally stopped she sensed all was not well. Why was there nobody to meet them? Fedutenko climbed out of the cockpit and looked around the lonely airstrip.

In the distance she made out a group of armed men running toward her. Immediately it hit her. "Nazis!" In an instant she jumped back into her aircraft and gave the engines full power for liftoff. There was no time to worry that she was taking off with the wind, only to get airborne before it was too late. As the aircraft clawed upward it almost brushed the heads of the bewildered enemy, who, frustrated in their attempt to capture the Russian machine intact with its crew, opened fire with a fusillade of automatic weapons, spraying it liberally with bullets.

Later Fedutenko joked that that episode was a landing into the very devil's teeth and her technicians back at base counted forty-seven bullet holes in her aircraft. She continued such exploits in the civilian aircraft group until she was commissioned into the air force and transferred to the Raskovoy Regiment of Pe-2 dive-bombers. Here she saw immense action, making nearly two hundred sorties and sometimes undertaking two or three combat dive-bombing missions a day.

As befitted her experience and war record to date, Fedutenko was appointed squadron leader of dive-bombers in this regiment. Her biographer and fellow flyer, Colonel N. Desnisov, was later to describe exactly what occurred:

> In those days I did not expect that I would fly into battle with her more than once. With such famous dive bomber pilots as Nadia, Lelia Sholochova, Shenya Timofeva, we, young and green pilots, looked up to [them] with great respect. They had a huge flying experience behind them, and we 18-year-old girls had seen nothing of life yet. We prepared long and hard for the front. Our older friends had already fought with the enemy but we had only heard about it with some jealousy. At last though, schooling and training was finished and we found ourselves at the frontline airfield.
>
> In the Regiment we met with some skepticism. Men pilots could not imagine that some girls as well as they could have mastered such a complicated technique as dive bombing and that we would be able to carry out combat missions and battle tasks efficiently. But after our first flights they were convinced that we could fly, not only as well as themselves, but sometimes even better.
>
> I particularly remember our first flight into battle. The honour of leading fell on our crew—I, with Nadia Fedutenko and Timofeva with Valentina Kravchenko. We were joined to the nine aircraft of another regiment to give us a chance to get familiar with the battle concepts in company of experienced pilots. How worried I was before the flight! All the calculations had been made, the orders were given and the planes were soon rolling out ready for take-off.

Nadia herself was so confident and assured in the air that I too began to reflect this feeling myself. Below us lay the burned, but not surrendered hero-city [Stalingrad, now Volgagrad]. When our bombs fell on the heads of the hated enemy we got the feeling of a truly fulfilled task. "Target destroyed," and thus the final victory comes another step closer. Anti-aircraft shells followed and surrounded us but we all returned safely to base.

On the same day our regiment got another order. The three best air crews, acting together with a group of the neighbouring regiment, were to deliver a blow on a surrounded group of enemy soldiers in the northern part of Stalingrad. Nadia Fedutenko led the attack of course and we duly unloaded 1,200 kilos of bombs directly on the heads of the Nazis. On many later missions together with Nadia Fedutenko we dive bombed German strongpoints, artillery and infantry positions in the Crimea and in the Kiev districts. More than once we had to fight our way through a storm of anti-aircraft fire and to beat off attacks by enemy fighters.

I remember one such incident, on 26 May 1943. We had been given the task of destroying enemy artillery positions in the Kiev district. In spite of the strong curtain of anti-aircraft fire over our targets, we stubbornly went on to carry out our bombing. Suddenly our aircraft was sharply shaken, it turned its nose downwards and started a steeper dive. But Nadia quickly managed to get it flying straight and true once more. I looked over at her and noticed that there was blood streaming from under her helmet and flowing down her face.

I immediately realized she had a head wound. We were only a few seconds from the target and Nadia noticed my worried expression and concern and said, "It is nothing, I will withstand it. You just make sure you aim more precisely." Once the bombs had been dropped fires started in the target zone and the enemy batteries were silenced. Fighting her pain Nadia led our return to base and calmly and confidently landed her aircraft and reported the successful completion of her task. Only after that had been done did she allow herself to be taken away to the hospital.

For this attack, a very precise and effective blow which assured the advance of our infantry, we received, while still in the air, the signals of gratitude of the Army commander of our ground forces.[1]

For this mission Fedutenko was awarded her first major citation— the Order of War for the Fatherland, First Class. Soon she resumed command of her Pe-2 squadron at the front and continued the fight. In the summer of 1944 during the great Russian offensive, severe fighting took place in the regions of Ozsha, Vitebsk, and Bozisov. Here the Soviet dive-bomber regiments flew intensive combat missions, again mounting up to three sorties in a single day.

Fedutenko was wounded a second time during the fighting in the region of Dvinsk when her copilot was Tosia Zubkova. However, even this second wound failed to daunt her spirit and she survived once again. She continued combat flying until the end of the war, taking her place proudly in the victory parade flypast over Moscow to mark their victory in the Great Patriotic War, as the Soviets call their part in World War II. Fedutenko thus became one of the very few pilots to earn the coveted distinction of being made Hero of the Soviet Union twice. It was an honor that she shared with that other outstanding Pe-2 dive-bomber pilot, Ivan Polbin.

Colonel Polbin commanded the 150th Bomber Air Regiment and his elite pilots became so proficient at precision bombing that they were known as "snipers" by the infantry. In just four days of fighting in defense of Stalingrad in August 1942, this regiment's aircraft destroyed forty German tanks and fifty motor vehicles.

The Soviets had also learned painful lessons in close air support, or "frontal aviation" as they termed it. Major General Fedor Falaleyev became chief of staff of the army air force during this critical period. He rapidly came to the conclusion that the German method of concentration at the vital spot instead of dispersal of available forces was the correct one. In July 1942, a directive was issued by the Russian Air Command. This directive pointed out: "Frontal Aviation employment in an offensive operation must be based on the most decisive concentration of aviation in the sector of the main troop thrust, and it must be employed in a limited number of combat missions. Operations were to be conducted in secondary sectors and in support of secondary troop missions only to the extent permitted by the availability of untasked aviation resources."[2]

It also added that:

> Such support would be possible only through centralized control of all aviation, which should not be taken to an extreme or become an end in itself. The tendency of some senior commanders to take charge [during] the operations of all units, even down to individual flights and planes, to completely exclude initiative on the part of junior commanders, could in no way be justified. It was recommended to air army commanders that aviation combat actions be supported by extensive air reconnaissance and observation over the battlefield; it was also recommended that

when planning combat actions, the commander should designate an aviation reserve which would be committed to battle at the decisive moment.[3]

The Il-2 for example, operating best at low levels, was initially not well received in traditional Soviet bomber units. Not until air crews had adapted to the merits of the aircraft and proven them in fighting conditions did it become the darling of the Eastern Front. We need them more than bread, Stalin hectored the Shturmovik builders. Likewise, the introduction of the highly advanced Petlyakov Pe-2 Peshka into the Soviet Union armory initially caused a few headaches. It was both technically and aerodynamically far advanced beyond what had gone before in this field. This meant difficulties in production, which were complicated further by the shift of the factories beyond the Ural Mountains for safety. Another problem was providing skilled crews to do justice to the aircraft itself.

The establishment of the *Pikiruyuschchii Bombardirovshchik* (dive-bomber) regiments began to take place early in 1941 and by the end of that year, some 1,869 had been produced. Such was their success that a grand total of 11,426 Pe-2 aircraft were built by the end of the war and 75 percent of all the Soviet twin-engine bomber squadrons were equipped with Pe-2 aircraft in 1945.

As usual, outstanding ground-attack pilots came to the fore in the harsh testing ground of war. These pilots tended to have the natural flair and feel for close support. Such individual aircrew expertise was a valued asset for combat flying, but the war on the Eastern Front was of such vast dimensions that it was necessary for mass to be coupled with such expertise. Traditional level bombers could not deliver the accuracy required, so the necessity of training the rapidly expanding ground-attack air regiments to a high degree of skill was recognized.

Another outstanding Soviet pilot, Colonel A. G. Fedorov, was directed by Colonel (later Lieutenant General) N. I. Krolenko, deputy chief of staff on the VVS (*Voyenno-Vozdushnyye Sily,* or air force) to draw up an official working paper for the correct use of the dive-bomber units. This paper incorporated Ivan Polbin's work to date. Practical testing was conducted by Fedorov himself on the bombing ranges but the final test came in battle. It was Fedorov who led a special Pe-2 regiment into action against German tanks and artillery in the area of Roslav. The first flight of three Peshki concentrated in 60-degree dives against the German flak guns to keep them busy while the other aircraft formed the carousel. The tactic worked, and not until it was repeated a second time did the enemy comprehend it. By then it was too late and accurate bomb-

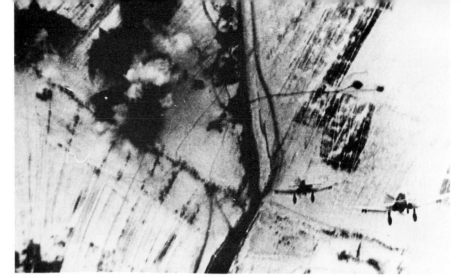

"When we say down, we mean STRAIGHT down," dive-bomber pilots used to say, but few actually dived at 90 degrees. Here the Stukas of St.G 77 show how it should be done as they dive onto a Soviet tank column caught out in the open steppe of the Eastern Front near Winniza during the bleak winter of 1943–44. (Author's collection, via Sellhorn)

The cockpit of a Vultee Vengeance dive-bomber of the RAF. This layout had been designed by Vultee in conjunction with the RAF pilots to provide the maximum ease and accessibility of operational functions so that the pilot was not distracted during his attack dive. When the USAAC took over these machines they found this layout did not fit its own standard specifications and thus modified it, much to the detriment of the Vengeance. (Author's collection, courtesy of Northrop Archives)

ing had been conducted. This confirmed the correctness of Polbin's Vertushka technique.

Thus in machines, hardware, and, finally, application, the Soviet ground-attack squadrons had, by 1943, become a very formidable machine indeed. The Germans, meanwhile, began to overextend, not just on the Eastern Front but elsewhere in Europe as well.

Across the Atlantic the sensational results of the Stukas in Europe in the summer of 1940 had an enormous impact. The US Air Corps was undergoing a vigorous expansion program under the leadership of General of the Army Henry Hap Arnold. They were still totally committed to the attack type and, as we have seen, these had progressively become larger and larger. The current model then in production was the Douglas A-20. Douglas knew how to build dive-bombers, as they had shown with the SBD Dauntless for the navy, but the A-20A was not intended for that role.

In June 1940 the Material Division had to advise that it was better to either adapt existing navy dive-bombers or create their own rather than attempt to redesign the army A-20. General Arnold called for the establishment of "at least two groups of dive-bombers to operate with armored divisions" on the German model.[4]

Thus the "2181" program originally contained an urgent order for two hundred SBD-2 Dauntless dive-bombers, and negotiations with Douglas commenced accordingly. In the end they decided to procure only seventy-eight A-24s (as the army classified the SBD) initially and revert back to A-20 bombers. This was with the proviso that the A-24 aircraft "would be capable of dive, glide or horizontal bombing,"[5] despite their earlier resolution!

Seventy-eight navy Douglas SBDs became the army air corps' Banshee as an immediate short-term solution while negotiations were started with the navy and Curtiss to procure an army version of the new SB2C Helldiver then in production as the new army dive-bomber, again adopting the name of Shrike. Under project B-71, $1,832,000 was set aside for development of the type.

Under these emergency plans of 1940 the army set itself two immediate tasks. First, they had to establish exactly what was required to enable navy dive-bombers to use air corps bombs and other equipment. Second, they wanted engineering studies to modify the A-20 type airplane so that it was capable of dive-, glide-, and horizontal bombing. As we have seen, this proved impracticable.

The US Army eventually ordered five different types of dive-bomber, three as adaptations of navy types and two brand-new designs. Of these the Banshees saw limited combat but were abandoned after heavy losses in the southwest Pacific in 1942. The new Shrike never got far beyond the design stage due to continual modification problems, and the American-built variant of the British-ordered Vultee Vengeance (A-35) were also so long delayed that they were finally not used in combat by the United States. Another of the brand-new types that was aborted before it began as far as the United States Army Air Force was concerned was the A-34. Initially 140 of these machines, the Brewster SB2A-1 Buccaneer, were asked for (750 were also ordered for the Royal Navy as the Bermuda, 140 for the US Navy, and 162 for the Dutch government. These latter aircraft for Holland were never delivered). Again building problems finished it off as other than a trainer and target tug.

Eventually only the dive-bomber version of the North American Mustang long-range fighter was a success in United States usage as a close-support machine. These aircraft, the A-24 "Apaches," were very advanced machines, but only five hundred were built. They saw considerable combat in the Mediterranean and Burma.

The seemingly endless production problems relating to the various dive-bomber projects caused unacceptable delays in getting them into service. This fact was coupled with the poor results and high losses of the few A-24s that the United States Air Force did finally manage to fly. Efforts were made to get some aircraft off the static production lines, but attempts to exchange types with the navy only caused more problems.

The end of all US Army interest in conventional dive-bombers came about at a conference held at Wright Field on 19 March 1943. The conference was to decide between the fighter-bomber or the dive-bomber approach for future close-support aircraft orders and combat deployments. The main points being considered were the advantages each type could offer in respect to forward machine or cannon fire in the traditional strafing role of the attack plane; the accuracy of each type to place a bomb on the target in a dive attack; ease of maintenance in the field; and, finally, speed at low altitudes.

They also took into account vulnerability to opposing fighter aircraft, the ability to take evasive action, and accuracy at the target compared to the fighter-bomber types (A-36, P-51, and P-39).

The conference concluded that fighter-bombers could better protect themselves against hostile fighter action by their speed and other fighter characteristics. It concluded that these types should be used with the N-3A modified gunsight in low-level as well as dive-bombing, but that specialized dive-bombers were not an army air force necessity.

The war in the Far East, which had commenced with the Japanese navy attack on Pearl Harbor in December 1941, had brought Japan and the United States into the shooting war while all this experimentation and theory was taking place. In the reality of war, practical considerations had to override theory.

The Japanese had already satisfied themselves as to what close-support aircraft they required and had built them in sufficient numbers to do the job. Although the main thrust of their sweeping conquests from Hong Kong to the Philippines, the Dutch East Indies, Malaya, Singapore, and on to the southwest Pacific relied on close cooperation between the navy dive-bombers and the landing forces, it was mainly an amphibious operation. Certainly close support was an integral part of their step-by-step advance on Australia and India, but usually opposing defenses were either poor or nonexistant. More often than not it was a

case of bombing the airfields and walking in to occupy them rather than making intensive air attacks in conjunction with land forces.

This is not to say that close air support did not feature in all the Japanese land conquests. Indeed it did. The Kawasaki Ki-32 "Mary" was present at the fall of Hong Kong. In the Philippines, American P-40s of the 17th and 34th Pursuit Squadrons bombed the Japanese beachhead at Vigan on 10 December using both fragmentation bombs and machine-gun strafing. Each P-40 could carry six of these 30-pound weapons under its wings. On the Japanese side, the Mitsubishi Ki-30 light bombers were deployed once American fighter defenses had been beaten down. The navy's Mitsubishi Zero fighters, having emptied the skies of American planes, spent their subsequent time in ground-strafing missions. One American defender of Nielson Field recorded: "I get awful upset by the bombing—the strafing is worst though. It's deadly. The bombing just scares you and the strafing kills you."[6]

Japanese navy dive-bombers were also effective. On 30 December they attacked Lubao railway sidings three times. Walter D. Edmonds wrote: "There were eight cars on the siding, and a train of forty cars stood idle on the main line. The Japanese got several hits on the eight cars, one of which caught fire. It was loaded with ammunition and soon began to explode.

"Betsy D" all bombed up but with its engine still needing attention. The A-36 (named the "Apache" or the "Invader" at various times of its life) was the dive-bomber version of the North American Mustang and was a sweet airplane to fly in vertically by all accounts. The planes were employed in North Africa and covered the invasions of Pantelleria, Sicily, and Salerno before taking part in the long slog up the Italian mainland in 1943–44. Others were used on the borders of India, Burma, and China in Southeast Asia, operating from hidden airstrips deep in the jungle. (George Halliwell)

Two Japanese army Ki-44 "Sonia" bombers in action over British Malaya early in 1942 in the lightning campaign that led to the fall of Singapore, the "Impregnable Fortress," a few weeks later. (Author's collection)

"Ammunition was exploding briskly among the eight cars on the siding, and the eighteenth car of the long train was burning hard."[7]

These railroad cars contained the only ammunition to be salvaged for the American defenders, and without it the American cause was a lost one.

In Malaya the Japanese army used four *sentais* (squadrons) equipped with both the Kawasaki Ki-44 and Ki-48 light bombers, and in Burma the Japanese used these aircraft wisely and economically to achieve their objectives. The Allies had nothing but conventional light bombers with which to oppose them, and once again these proved totally ineffective. Air Chief Marshal Sir Robert Brooke-Popham, the AOC Malaya, was heard to relate: "Every week I ask London for three things, torpedo planes, dive bombers and tanks."[8]

He was to receive none of these; instead Blenheim light bombers were flown out from the Middle East to substitute. They were the standard RAF answer to pleas for ground-support aircraft. They were gallantly flown and heroically sacrificed. And they were utterly useless.

Like the Japanese attacks, most of the hastily adapted British fighter-bomber or light bomber sorties were directed against maritime targets, invasion convoys, or battle fleets rather than flown in direct support of troops on the ground. Exceptions were the makeshift use of P-40Es as fighter-bombers in the Philippines and similar dive-bomber conversions of Commonwealth Wirraway trainers during the Malayan debacle.

In Java, Japanese navy dive-bombers caught and obliterated five B-17 Flying Fortress bombers at Malang airfield. The only flak defenses they had to face were old French 75 artillery pieces which the Dutch 131st Field Artillery elevated as high as they could, but which had no effect.

The US 27th Bombardment Squadron with twenty A-24 Banshees (minus solenoids, gunsights, armor protection, and self-sealing fuel tanks, and with defective rear mountings and worn-out tires, due to the rush to get them shipped out to the war zone) was hastily assembled at Archer Field in Australia. Three more Banshees from the 91st Bombardment Squadron arrived at Darwin airfield on 10 February only to be shot to bits by the Australian antiaircraft gunners there! All somehow got down, but only one remained in flying condition.

On 19 February two A-24s made the first dive-bombing attack in the history of the US Army. They claimed to have sunk a destroyer and a transport. In fact, analysis of postwar records clearly shows that no Japanese ship was actually sunk.

In Burma the Japanese advance threatened to spread across the Chinese western border via the Salween Gorge. Missions by the American Volunteer Groups P-40E fighters fitted with makeshift bomb racks to carry a single 500-pound bomb proved highly effective in stopping the Japanese column and then devastating it. Hemmed in the narrow defile, the enemy troops were then systematically strafed by the "Flying Tigers" and the invasion threat was lifted. Here was close air support deployed in a strictly tactical role having a strategical effect far beyond its immediate mission. Unfortunately, little attention was paid to it.

Not until 1943 did more serious close-support work take place in the Eastern combat zones. American and Australian air forces began striking hard at Japanese troops in Papua, New Guinea, as the Australians and Americans first halted then threw back the Japanese jungle columns heading for Port Moresby. The Australians and Americans employed Commonwealth Wirraway trainers as dive-bombers and also Kittyhawk fighter-bombers, Bristol Beaufighters, all twin-engine machines, as well as limited strikes by Banshees, Airacobras, and later A-20 Havocs in low-level strafing and fragmentation bomb configurations.

The Japanese navy accepted the prime responsibility for helping the Japanese army in this area and mainly contented itself with dive-bomber attacks against specific targets from land bases in the Rabaul, New Britain, area, supplemented from time to time by intensive operations by the carrier-borne squadrons. Both types were carried out by the Aichi "Val" dive-bomber, but long-range strikes against American marines moving into Guadalcanal and the Solomons proved a waste as the short-legged dive-bombers did not have the fuel to complete the round trip.

In the Solomons campaigns of 1942–43 close support was provided very effectively by the Douglas Dauntless dive-bombers of the US Marine Corps and navy fliers, working from shore from the much-disputed

To oppose the relentless advance of the Japanese in New Guinea the RAAF was forced to use whatever aircraft were available. The Commonwealth Wirraway proved itself adaptable as a dive-bomber and was thus employed in limited strikes until other aircraft became available. Here a Wirraway of No. 4 Squadron is being armed with underwing 250-pound bombs. (Australian War Memorial, Canberra ACT)

With a powerful armament of cannon, machine guns, and rocket projectiles, the Bristol Beaufighter of the RAF was an extremely potent ground-attack weapon. In the Far East its efficiency in this role earned for it the respected title of "Whispering Death" from the Japanese troops in Burma and Southeast Asia. (Imperial War Museum, London)

Although the Imperial Japanese Navy used its Aichi "Val" dive-bombers as one of the main arms of its carrier squadrons in the great naval battles of the Pacific war between 1941 and 1945, they were also extensively deployed from island air bases in the South Pacific war zone, operating mainly from the Rabaul area in direct support of Japanese military forces defending the Solomons and New Guinea. (Author's collection)

Henderson Field on Guadalcanal, and also from aircraft carriers at sea. But again priority was given to attacking Japanese naval targets.

In 1941–42 then, the Germans had all the correct ingredients for the application of efficient close air support. The Soviets had good aircraft for the job, but poorly trained pilots, poor communications, and no proper plans. The Americans had few proper aircraft and little practical experience, but enormous potential to produce both given time. The British were still largely disinterested and clung stubbornly to the old-formation, high-level bombing in idea, although that was ultimately to change. Meanwhile they were briskly bundled out of Libya by Rommel using a few Stukas and Panzers against which they still had no effective counter.

A British air marshal could still write as late as 1943, and in the face of all the evidence, that:

> It is true that the enemy have been using dive bombers from the beginning and that they have been successful when employed under conditions suitable to their highly specialised characteristics.
>
> The idea that the dive bomber will obtain an effective proportion of hits against, for example, moving tanks is not justified by any experience of which the Air Staff have been informed.
>
> It is understood that the Russians possess dive bombers but information as to the use they have made of them is scanty. We have no information that they have proved as useful to the Russians as the Germans in their propaganda claim they have been to them (the Germans). The *Stormovic* [sic] is used mainly as a low level attack aircraft. It is understood that the Mustang was to be produced in a version fitted with brakes but there is not information that any such aircraft have been employed in operations. The bombing so far done by Mustangs has been of the fighter-bomber kind.[9]

All of which was totally at variance with the facts!

The RAF response was still in the good old British tradition that a keen amateur was always a better bet than a dedicated professional. "It is true that we have nothing like the specialised ground-attack structure employed by the Germans, but the light bombers employed in the desert, Blenheims and Bostons, have proved most effective in slowing down enemy advances."[10]

Moreover, many shared Winston Churchill's puzzlement at the continuing defeats in the desert despite the strident claims of the Air Ministry that the RAF controlled the desert skies:

> People fail to understand how it can be said, as was stated by General Auchinleck, that we maintained moral superiority in the air while at the same time we were unable to stop the advance. This leads to doubts as to the availability of the correct aerial weapons, and has again raised the whole question of dive bombers and other questions as to type of aircraft. There is in this sphere an uneasiness that the outlook is too rigid as regards types and that this rigidity is preventing us, even with air superiority, from being as effective in fighting from the air as the enemy.[11]

It was mainly in the North African desert campaigns of 1941–43 that the Royal Air Force close-support squadrons came into contact with the German and Italian land forces and could demonstrate their effectiveness, or otherwise. The fighting was all on a small scale compared with the Russian front and thus the Germans never had many more than seventy Junkers Ju 87D Stukas as their main close-support machines. To these were added twenty to thirty Italian-manned Stukas and various Bf 190 Jabo units.

Despite the smallness of their numbers, the Luftwaffe managed to organize their close air support far more effectively than the numerically superior British and later Allied air forces for the first two years of the desert war. Stukas were as often as not switched from the land war to attack British convoys steaming to Malta. Although they caused heavy losses to both merchant ships and escorting warships alike, this tended to divert them from the 8th Army, thus enabling the British soldiers to escape from nasty situations. For example, in June 1942 all the Luftwaffe's ground support aircraft were sent against a supply convoy bound for Malta over a three-day period. This coincided with the rout of the British army back to El Alamein. The coastal roads were packed with motor transport and would have been ideal Stuka bait. The British army commander later sent his sincere thanks to the RAF for preventing their being "Stukad" to bits. The RAF claimed (yet again) this to be the death knell of the dive-bomber. The plain facts and truth of this affair was that the Germans' dive-bombers had been sent out to attack a British convoy to Malta out at sea during this period. The Stukas caused heavy losses to the convoy, and the ships turned back, but it was this fortunate deployment of the Stukas against the ships rather than the RAF fighters to which the British army's retreat owed its relative immunity.

When Rommel took Tobruk 20 June 1942 he employed dive-bombers in a very special way. At 0600 three waves totaling 120 Ju 87s attacked the southeastern perimeter. They hit hard, not directly at the 11th Indian Brigade's defense positions, but at the surrounding minefields. The dive-bombers thus blasted a clear path through for the Panzers in a unique variation of close support, and German tanks were patrolling the streets of the town before the British commander knew they had pierced his defenses!

The Italians also continued to employ the Junkers Ju 87D but found that the Fiat Cr.42 biplane and later the Macchi MC 200 monoplane fighter could both be adapted for the ground-strafing role with their Stormo Assalto units. These fought in all the major land campaigns from "Crusader" to El Alamein.

Nonetheless it was in North Africa that British, and later American, ground-attack aircraft and methods were first tried out in combat. It was here that tactics were first employed that no longer relied on the Bristol Blenheim and Douglas Boston twin-engine medium bombers. Also, the German air controllers' system was adopted by the RAF and improved upon.

The first steps were the modification of the older single-engine fighter aircraft to carry both bombs and high-velocity 40-mm tank-busting cannon. The first tests of the ability of the Hawker Hurricane IIA to carry a pair of 250-pound general purpose (GP) bombs were not made until early 1941. Almost another year passed before the IIB and IIC Hurricanes were so fitted, the latter having four 20-mm Oerlikon cannon to back up the bombs while later models adopted the Hispano cannon for this job. Nos. 1 and 3 Squadrons employed these machines on low altitude intruder missions over the Channel, known as "rhubarbs." The twin-engine Westland Whirlwind fighter aircraft with four cannon in its nose was similarly employed from mid 1941 onward. Finally, the adoption of the Curtiss Kittyhawks and North American Mustangs also strengthened and fitted for bomb carrying completed a series of fighter-bomber adaptations.

Among the earliest Allied fighter aircraft adapted for dive-bombing and close-support bombing was the North American P-51 Mustang. Because of its poor fighter performance at high altitudes, the RAF had initially used the Mustang in the low-level role. As a fighter-bomber the Mustang proved capable of carrying two 500-pound bombs with ease and of delivering them to the target with skill and accuracy. (Imperial War Museum, London)

Although not as sturdy as the custom-built dive-bomber, the single-seat fighter was capable of lifting heavier and heavier bomb loads as the war progressed. As enemy fighter opposition waned suitable employment of such interceptors was found in the close air support role. Here "Cleopatra III," a Curtiss P-40 Kittyhawk flown by Wing Commander Atherton of No. 80 Squadron, RAAF, with his wingman just visible behind and below, lugs ordnance comprising fused 250-pound bombs over the Southwest Pacific en route to another Japanese strongpoint. (Australian War Memorial, Canberra ACT)

To use them in support of troops in European combat was out of the question, but the desert air force was crying out for such a weapon. Under the leadership of Air Marshal Sir Arthur Coningham, commander of the Desert Air Force and later the North African Tactical Air Force, the German method of sending specialized communication teams of air force officers forward with the army columns as forward air controllers (FAC) was adopted by the British. Like the Germans and the Russians, they found that the stricter the control and the tighter the network, the more effective the support became.

It was in November 1941 that the very first British fighter-bomber squadron, No. 80 flying old Hurricane I machines fitted with eight 40-pound fragmentation bombs under the wings, made its debut. By the end of January it had reconverted to the fighter role once more! In March 112 Squadron with Curtiss P-40Es was experimenting with dropping 250-pound bombs and in May it became the first Kittybomber squadron. At the same time the Hawker Hurricane IID arrived in the Middle East with No. 6 Squadron. Fitted with two Vickers 40-mm "S" guns under the wings, each with fifteen rounds, it was to prove a formidable antitank weapon. Its power was strictly offensive, for it lacked any armor protection for the pilot.

In the heavy fighting of June 1942 the RAF was deploying two Kittybomber and one Hurribomber squadron, all carrying 250-pound bombs to good effect, and these were steadily reinforced throughout the rest of that year. No. 6 Squadron was effective but after intensive fighting was withdrawn to rest, leaving no cannon-carrying fighters until it returned in company with 7 Squadron South African air force in time for El Alamein.

Although the bulk of the German close-support aircraft was employed in Russia, the Allied ground advances into French Tunisia in November 1942 found that the handful of Stukas that remained could still upset their apple cart. A few of the armored Henschel Hs 129Bs were also flown in by SG2, but their Gnome-Rhone engines were made largely unserviceable by the sand and dust of the region and they did not shine.

As the Allies advanced, the bridge at Medjez-el-Bad assumed vital importance to both the Germans and Allies alike. The defending French troops were hastily reinforced by a British parachute battalion and a US field battalion. These troops, some 3,500 men in all, were outbluffed by only three hundred German paratroops under Captain Helmut Koche. The Germans fought so hard that the Allies convinced themselves that they were up against several thousand men. Basil Liddell Hart related what followed: "An hour and a half later German dive bombers came on the scene to add punch to the bluff. Following up the dive-bombing attacks, which shook the defenders badly, the German paratroopers made two small ground attacks, and that air of vigorous effect created an exaggerated impression of their strength. That night the Germans occupied Medjez-el-Bad."[12]

It is interesting to note the effect that just two score Junkers Ju 87 dive-bombers (now three years past their claimed demise in the Battle of Britain) had on both British and American ground forces in the Tunisian campaign. Daniel R. Mortensen, in the definitive study of the campaign, states: "The greatest problem, according to the ground commanders, was the repeated attack by the supposedly obsolete German Stukas. Fighters would be called up for defensive cover, but because of the great distances, the fighter loitering time was brief. While the Allied aircraft were in the air, German dive bombers merely returned to their airfields and waited for the all-clear signals. Allied air forces could not provide enough continuity in their air cover."[13]

General Dwight D. Eisenhower himself stated that German "strafing and dive-bombing" were responsible for stopping the attempted advances of the First Army. Lieutenant General Kenneth Anderson went further, stating baldly that unless German attacks of this type could be reduced, the Allied ground forces would have to withdraw to a position where they could get cover.

The climax in Tunisia came for the RAF fighter-bombers on 26 March 1943, when no fewer than eighteen squadrons of these close-support airplanes were deployed to help the armies force their way through the Tebaga Gap. They lost fifteen of their number in one day of continual low-level attacks against German artillery positions defending the vital road to El Hamma, but they served their purpose. The Tunisian campaign also marked the nadir for the Hurricane IID squadrons. No. 6 Squadron, for example, lost sixteen aircraft to German flak gunners in just five days' operations. No armored ground-attack aircraft were ever produced for the RAF or the USAAF despite repeated pleas for such machines by their respective armies.

six

Expansion and Limitations

By the final two years of the war the pattern of close air support had been firmly established. For the innovators, Germany, it was now a defensive war with the bulk of their commitment, both on land and in the air, in the East. Their army cooperation planning had peaked at the Battle of Kharkov in February 1943. Both the new Henschel Hs 129 with its 75-mm cannon and six-tube 75-mm rocket launcher and the Ju 87 G with its twin 37-mm cannon were employed to good effect against the hordes of Soviet T 34s belonging to the Soviet 3d Tank Army. They caught this formation in middeployment on the open steppe and attacked, creating havoc. The entire tank army was decimated.

Similar tactics were employed that same July against the Kursk salient and the Panzer Jager squadrons, but this time the enemy were dug in and ready. The close-support aircraft had the added hazards of flying across the curtains of artillery shells between the two armies. Losses were heavy on both sides but after three days the Soviets launched their counterstroke preceded by wave upon wave of Il-2 Shturmoviks now equipped with 37-mm cannon. In one day, 7 July, 17 Panzer Division was under continuous "Circle of Death" attacks for four hours by these aircraft and lost 240 of its 300 tanks. Similar slaughter was done to both 3 and 9 Panzer Divisions, which lost 270 and 70 tanks respectively to air attack that day.

The Soviet 2 Tank Army counterattacked north of Belgordo the next day and was in turn caught by the Luftwaffe. I and II/SchG1 and 4 and 8/SchG 2 equipped with Hs 129s were sent in to make repeated attacks.

They were backed up by FW 190s Jabos with their cannon and SD1 and SD2 canisters which hit the supporting Soviet infantry. This smashed the attack with an estimated destruction of fifty T34s.

The Germans employed their mixed Stuka units in a plan evolved by the master tank-killer of all time, Major Hans-Ulrich Rudel. Using this method the bomb-carrying Ju 87Ds went for the enemy antiaircraft defenses, swamping them with bomb and strafing attacks. This left the way open for the Panzer Jager Staffeln to make their approaches from the rear of the target at between 15 and 25 feet, where their unprotected engines lay wide open to the tungsten-tipped shells. Using this method Rudel personally destroyed more than five hundred Soviet tanks and scores of lesser vehicles.

It was by the valiant and unceasing efforts of the Junkers Ju 87 aircraft that the huge Soviet enveloping thrusts north and east of Orel were finally contained and an even greater disaster than Stalingrad averted. It was a famous victory for ground-attack aircraft, but it was to be the Germans' last. To coordinate all the various branches of Luftwaffe close-support units, a new post was created: Waffengeneral de Schlachtflieger. The five existing Hs 129B units were to be combined as IV (Panzer)/SG 9 led by Bruno Meyer, but constant enemy pressure up and down the whole of the Eastern Front prevented them from ever operating in this manner.

All the main *Stukageschwader* (Stuka Wings), 1, 2, 3, and 77, became *Schlachtgeschwader* (Ground Attack Wings) and the various Jabo units also merged into Schlacht formations.

Night attack squadrons known as the *Nachtschlachtgruppen* were formed. These new units were equipped with obsolete Stukas which had been retired from day combat sorties and replaced by Focke-Wulf Fw 190 Jabos. The bomb loads that could be carried by the latest models of this fighter, F and G, increased to 2,200 pounds (SC1000) or a combination of 250-pound and 550-pound weapons. The Fw190 also mounted two 20-mm cannon and machine guns. All this was combined with a top speed of 340 mph.

The attack method employed by these aircraft was to approach at 7,000 feet in two groups, each in turn making diving attacks at a 70-degree angle with bomb release at 1,000 feet and following up with a strafing run.

But after Kursk the Germans' effort was a waning one. They were simply swamped by the enormous flood of new tanks and close-support

aircraft the Soviets were able to deploy. Ground-attack units were switched desperately from one crumbling front to another and on frequent occasions scored outstanding local success. But they could not stop the overall trend of events by themselves. Although warplanes flew until the last day of the war, the Luftwaffe could never again dominate the land war as it had between 1939 and 1942.

On the Soviet side, they had now established their tactics and it remained only to steadily and surely improve both the quantity of their existing aircraft types and the training of their air crews to use them to the maximum effect. The Pe-2s steadily increased the scope of their precision attacks until this dive-bomber's speed and versatility made it the main close-support aircraft by the end of the war. Meanwhile the much-feared Il-2 was employed in overwhelming numbers, and an improved version, the Il-10, appeared. In the final great battles between 1944 and 1945 as many as three thousand Soviet aircraft were deployed over some sectors of the front as the Soviet offensives ground steadily toward and then over the German frontier.

The Russians were slower to use fighter-bombers as they were used by their German opponents or in the West because of this growing strength of their specialized ground-attack machines. By the last year of the war, however, such was the preponderance of Soviet air power that they could afford the luxury of allowing single-engine fighters like the Yakovlev Yak 9B to carry four internally stacked 100-kilogram bombs. The Lavochkin La-7 could carry 440 pounds of bombs more conventionally under the wings and of course all were frequently utilized as ground strafers with 20-mm, 37-mm, and even 57-mm cannon as the opportunity arose.

Despite intensive efforts, no satisfactory, fully automatic dive-bombing sight was developed during World War II, and most pilots, Allied and Axis, relied on eye-sighting or elementary devices to sight their targets. In Sweden, however, a determined attempt was made to develop such a sight and was rewarded with success, but only after the war. By 1944–45 the Swedish air force, still relying on accuracy to make up for its lack of numbers, was using the SAAB S-18A twin-engine dive-bomber. This aircraft is from their F21 squadron fitted with an external radar dome under the cockpit. (Nils Kindberg, Stockholm)

Another weapon that became almost universally adopted in the West in the ground-attack role was the unguided rocket. The Soviets had, of course, pioneered such work and a larger version, the RS-132, began to be used. The German response was the Panzerschreck missile, an 88-mm rocket which was mounted in groups of three under each wing, and later a larger version, the Panzerblitz, was experimented with. Despite this, the aimed cannon still remained the most efficient and effective antitank weapon on both sides of the Eastern Front until the end of the war.

In the West the momentum remained in the Mediterranean area throughout 1943 and early 1944. Here the Americans started deploying the North American A-36A Invader dive-bomber to good effect attacking the defending forces in the islands of Pantelleria and Sicily and also during the invasion of mainland Italy at Salerno. This modification of the famous Mustang could carry two 500-pound bombs beneath the wings and was fitted with dive brakes. Although it is an article of faith with almost every postwar air historian that these aircraft were inevitably used in low-level attacks and not dive-bombing, and that they had the dive brakes "wired shut" in action, the pilots that actually flew them tell a totally different story. For example John B. Watson, a pilot with the 525th Fighter Bomber Squadron, USAAF at that time, said: "I do not recall participating in any mission, as a wingman or a flight leader, when the brakes were *not* used if the bomb run began between 8,000 and 12,000 feet and the dive was vertical."[1]

Other Allied aircraft employed against ground targets in this area included American P-40s and RAF Kittyhawks, all carrying underwing loads of 20-pound and 40-pound "frag" bombs, a pair of 250-pound general purpose bombs, or single 500-pound and 1,000-pound bombs.

The Axis riposte was delivered, most effectively, by German Focke-Wulf Fw190As, and by Italian Reggiane Re 2002 Ariete and Macchi MC202 fighter-bombers, but these flew very few combat missions against land targets, being mainly directed against the invasion fleets and landing craft.

As the fighting proceeded in its slow and painful way up the Italian mainland between 1943 and 1945, all manner of fighter aircraft were used in the ground-strafing and fighter-bomber role. The P-51 Mustangs gradually replaced combat losses in the A-36 squadrons, although the latter had to be revived to stop a German counterattack at Salerno in the autumn of 1943. The big twin-engine Lockheed P-38 Lightnings, with their powerful nose cannon, proved very effective. They could also carry up to four 500-pound bombs at a time. Republic P-47D Thunderbolts, fitted with launching tubes for 4.5-inch rockets as well as two

1,000-pound bombs, appeared late in 1944. The ageing Curtiss Kittyhawks were reinforced by the Supermarine Spitfires Vs of the RAF's Desert Air Force, now far from the desert. They carried 250-pound bombs in diving attacks for lack of any other employment, rail cuts and similar tactical targets occupying their resources.

The mountainous nature of the land frequently called for dive-bombing, but the numerous German flak batteries made this a hazardous operation, so flak-suppression missions were frequently flown.

Finally, in common with the then-current practice in northwest Europe, RAF types like the Hawker Hurricane IV and the Bristol Beaufighter took over with their 3-inch rocket projectiles, which they released in dives at a range of about 1,000 feet.

In Italy the Allies adopted the "Rover" system. Each of the army corps had attached to it a liaison HQ ("Rover Tentacles") of air personnel. They agreed with the generals on levels of air support for each proposed operation and allocated the squadrons accordingly. The American XII Tactical Air Command committed all their aircraft—A36s, P51s, and P470s—each day while the Desert Air Force kept back a prudent reserve for emergencies, but otherwise the system worked the same. The "Cab Rank" system of constant readiness in which patrols of fighter-bombers would be kept aloft with others bombed up and ready on the runways awaiting their own call to action.

The big, sturdy Republican P-47 Thunderbolts of the 9th US Air Force proved themselves highly efficient dive-bombing machines during the last year of the European conflict and could carry up to three 500-pound bombs on such missions. (Smithsonian Institution, Washington, DC)

Ultimately, with the near-demise of much of the German and Japanese fighter forces, the hugely expanded heavy fighter units of the Allies had little to do in their designed role. Fortunately most proved adaptable for ground-strafing and dive-bombing missions and many units spent almost their entire war service doing these jobs with great success.

P-51 Mustangs often operated at low levels, and they had the formidable range that made their reputation. At higher altitudes the enemy machines still had the edge, as the RAF found out early on. By 1945 the USAAF was also employing their P-51s (of various marks) on "seek and destroy" ground-attack missions using their cannon against retreating enemy columns. (Smithsonian Institution, Washington, DC)

Once each land battle reached a critical stage, the Forward Air Control Unit ("Rover David") coordinated requests from individual forward troops as well as reconnaissance flights over the front line. With an army major and an RAF flight lieutenant working together with a back-up team from both services, remarkable harmony was achieved. The information from aerial and ground reconnaissance was built on a grid reference system, similar to that used by the German U-boats in the North Atlantic, whereby each sector was cross-referenced from common squared maps and then passed up the line by direct VHF/RT to the appropriate Cab Rank.

This made for quick target location, and these units were fully mobile, the thirty-men teams and their various VHF and HF R/T sets being moved in large Quad tractor units supplemented by Scout cars and, of course, Jeeps.

While the Italian campaign gradually stagnated, attention shifted to France with the invasion of Normandy on 6 June 1944. Here the Allies deployed vast fleets of ground-support aircraft to great effect. The principal aircraft types were as already mentioned above but in far larger numbers. In addition, the famous 3-inch-rocket attacks by the RAFs 2d Tactical Air Force Hawker Typhoons became legendary. Carrying a 60-pound high explosive warhead or an armor-piercing shot, these weapons were not very accurate at anything beyond the 1,000-foot

After the breakout from the Normandy beachheads, the war in western Europe moved steadily toward the frontiers of the Reich. The outnumbered German tanks and soldiers, vastly more battle-experienced and resilient than those of the Allies, were largely nullified by the fighter-bombers of the Allied tactical squadrons. More and more the rocket became the precision weapon that culled Hitler's elite Panzer units and his dug-in infantry positions and ground them down.

The aircraft are British Hawker Typhoons of 2 TAF and the date is 22 February 1945. The German strongpoint is a fortified farmhouse west of Calcar. Two Typhoons can just be seen approaching this target. The leading aircraft has just released its rockets toward the strongpoint. The two white puffs in the center of the photograph show the point of release, with the smoke trails pointing at the target. The aircraft is just above the rockets and between the two beginnings of the smoke trails. The other aircraft is coming in to attack (extreme right). (Imperial War Museum, London)

range but, fired in salvos of eight at a time against tanks and soft-skinned vehicles alike, they gave each single-engine fighter the punch of a 6-inch light cruiser salvo. British Hawker Typhoons and American Thunderbolts were also employed in precision dive-bombing attacks while Mustangs ground-strafed rear-area transport. The Germans had little or no aerial defense but, as always, their flak was concentrated, accurate, and deadly.

It was probably for this reason that rockets were so popular with western close-support aviators and so widely used. They soon made an indelible mark on the Normandy fighting. On 7 August a German Panzer counterattack against Avranches and Vire stalled in the narrow hedged-in lanes and here they were gleefully pounced on by no less than nineteen squadrons of rocket-firing Typhoons. In a manner similar to the Nablus debacle of a quarter-century earlier, the RAF pilots struck at the rear and head of the tank columns around Mortain and then proceeded to methodically work them over. In all, 294 sorties were flown that day, during which more than 2,000 rockets were fired and 80 tons of bombs were dropped on the trapped Panzers. For the loss of only three aircraft, more than eighty German armored vehicles were destroyed, although whether by the rockets themselves or by subsequent cannon fire is still the subject of fierce debate. Whichever it was, the German attack was stopped cold.

In August it was the subsequent German withdrawal through the narrow Falaise Gap that gave the Typhoons a golden opportunity to add to their legend, and they duly took it. Once more German armor and soft-skinned vehicles were caught unable to maneuver in nose-to-tail jams by the Allied close-support aircraft. Reinforced by cannon-firing

During the German retreat through the Falaise Gap in Normandy during the late summer of 1944, Allied tactical air support came into its own. The orderly withdrawal was turned into a rout as the German armor and light transport, congested on the narrow French lanes, became sitting ducks for round-the-clock air strikes. It was the blitzkrieg in reverse.

Here an RAF Hawker Typhoon fires rockets at mobile targets caught on the road at Livarot. (Imperial War Museum, London)

and bomb-dropping Thunderbolts, Mustangs, Spitfires, and "Bomphoons," the rocket-firing Typhoons returned to the assault and another massacre resulted.

This set the pattern for the subsequent drive through the Low Countries and on the Rhine. Luftwaffe response was weak, but included jet-powered Messerschmitt Me262 fighter aircraft which were wasted and misused as "Blitz Bombers" with four MK 108 30-mm cannon and two SC 250-pound bombs under the fuselage. But their impact and that of the dwindling numbers of FW190 units was minimal.

The French navy provided some of the final close-support combat in western Europe. Capitane de Fregate Francis Laine had previous experience with dive-bombers which made him a natural selection for the post of commander of the Groupement Aeronavale 2, a brand-new unit forming at Algiers on 1 March 1944, with thirty-seven Douglas SBD Dauntless dive-bombers supplied by the Americans. Laine had to supervise the assembly of a new unit and its training and equipping. This time he had the help of the US Navy as well in getting started from scratch. Both 3F and 4F were originally to be assigned to the carrier *Bearn* but later Laine was told that his role had been switched. Once more the French navy dive-bombers were to operate as a land-based close-support unit, blasting the way ahead of the reconstructed French army and freeing German-occupied Paris. But by the time the unit was ready, Paris had fallen. However, strong German garrisons had retreated into their citadel fortresses along the Channel ports. Hitting the garrisons, which were interspersed with French civilian populations, required precision bombing. Typical Allied carpet bombing was out of the question as enormous loss of innocent life would have resulted. Only the dive-bombers could achieve the necessary accuracy.

Ironically, two years earlier, Allied air chiefs had disdained the use of dive-bombers for the invasion of Europe, calling them too vulnerable. They had firmly ruled out all possibilities of such aircraft being used. Now they had to eat their words. Their earlier nonsensical decision, which had been to not deploy such dive-bombers on European battlefields, had the incidental result of abandoning the Vultee Vengeance, with which the French squadrons were to have reequipped. Now, using instead the older, slower, and relatively more obsolete Douglas Dauntless, the French navy was called upon to take part in the European land war as a dive-bomber unit after all.

Their principal objectives were the German garrisons at Pointe de Graves, Royan, and La Rochelle. In October 1944, therefore, Laine's squadron became part of the Groupement Aeronvale 2 under Major Max de la Menardiere, which comprised the 3 and 4 Dive Bomber Flotilles and the Base Mobile No. 2, a total of eight hundred to one thousand men. This close-support unit was attached to the Armée de l'Atlantique commanded by General de Corps d'Armée de Larminat as part of 6 Army Group.

They were first called into action during the German offensive against the Americans around Bastogne in late 1944. Here the Dauntless were loaded up with 1,000-pound bombs, which almost proved too heavy for them, and were hastily sent against the German spearheads at the siege of Trianon Palace. In November and December 1944, 84 tons of bombs were dropped, another 60 tons were delivered in January, and 72 tons were dropped in March against enemy positions. From 31 March to 2 May Laine's SBDs were in almost daily action against the Channel ports and they also flew dive-bomber missions against German batteries on the Ile d'Oléron, which led to its liberation. Between 15 and 20 April, some 72 sorties were flown and 320 tons of bombs were dropped. In many of their precision attacks, so close were they to French civilian populations that the use of 1,000-pound bombs was forbidden and they had to dive-bomb with smaller bombs. These therefore had to be placed with some delicacy to ensure they did their job just as well. For his work in these highly successful missions Laine and 2 Flotille were awarded the Croix de Guerre with Palms at the end of April by recommendation of General Charles de Gaulle himself. It was presented by the president of the Republic.

We have already seen how the withdrawal of strong German land forces into their powerful fortresses of concrete and steel set in the French Channel ports of Pointe de Graves, Royan, La Rochelle, and Ile d'Oléron in the autumn of 1944 had forced the Allies to turn to the dive-bomber to blast them out. Such attacks required great care and precision due to the close proximity of the French civilian populations and buildings of historical importance. In conjunction with the French army, therefore, the Dauntless dive-bombers that equipped both French navy and French army air force squadrons conducted a long series of precision dive-bombing attacks from November 1944 until April 1945 (with a break while they were used to halt the German Ardennes offensive) that gradually whittled down these bastions one by one. It was a perfect example of controlled, accurate bombing and contrasted starkly with the area-bombing policies that had hitherto turned European cities into wastelands of debris from Brest to Berlin. It was far more economical in terms of manpower, ammunition, expense, and casualties, both civilian and military. From all of these missions over the six-month operational period the French navy lost only five of its dive-bombers, despite the renowned accuracy and skill of the German flak gunners. This in spite of repeated dire predictions to the contrary by high-ranking RAF officers from 1940 onward.

The first of the two units utilized in these attacks was of course the French navy's GAN2 Group, led by Capitaine de Fregate Francis Laine and based at Cognac. This Group had 3B under Lieutenant de Vaisseau Ortolan and 4B under Lieutenant de Vaisseau Behic. They flew numerous sorties between 9 December 1944 (with an attack on German batteries at Verdon) and 20 April 1945, dropping some 500 tons of bombs in 1,150 missions and 1,400 combat hours. A particularly effective attack delivered against the fortified village of Fontbedeau on the road to Royan totally obliterated the target. This accuracy was maintained throughout.

The second Dauntless squadron in action here was the French army GCBI/18 Vendee squadron, based at Vannes with sixteen A-24Bs Dauntless and led by Commandant Lapios. This unit was initially based at Toulouse airfield from September 1944 onward and took part in operations in the south of France before being transferred to Brittany. There it conducted missions similar to Laine's squadron, attacking German fortifications and strongpoints at Lorient and St. Nazaire. It lost a total of four aircraft during this five-month period of combat operations.

Admiral Francis Laine described the Dauntless in this manner: "The Douglas SBD was a very accurate weapons system. It certainly was not very fast (about 350 km/h) but it was well armed with heavy machine guns and provided a good loading platform for 500-kg and even larger bombs. Developed especially for naval warfare against Japan, it proved readily adaptable and was very good in attacking fixed land targets as well."[2]

The German flak defenses, which consisted of Fla.Abt. 999s, in the region of the Gironde were formidable indeed. It was estimated that these machines under Hauptmann Nolle could defend the estuary with over 33 pieces of 75-mm and 103 mountings of the famous quadruple 20-mm light flak guns. Moreover, the Germans had had four years to dig themselves in, concrete themselves over, and skillfully camouflage their positions. It availed them little. However, the weather on the Channel coast was not always favorable for precision dive-bombing attacks and on cloudy days opportunity for glory was rare.

The final battle to take the German fortress complex on the island of Oléron, which lay strategically to the north of the mouth of the Gironde opposite La Rochelle, the port serving Rochefort itself, was code-named Operation "Jupiter." Heavy bombardments by a French cruiser and three destroyers were followed by landings on 29 April, and combat ashore continued until 1 May before the Germans capitulated.

On 30 April 1945, during the fighting that followed the initial French landings planned to liberate the island, the morning dawned dull and heavily overcast. Because of this the French army commander in chief feared that the Germans at La Rochelle would ferry reinforcements across to the island garrison. The navy dive-bomber group was therefore asked to supply a division of SBDs to keep constant watch for such a German troop convoy and attack if it indeed materialized.

As Laine later said:

> Six aircraft of Flotille under Lieutenant de Vaisseau Ortolan took off to carry out this mission at 0600. They saw absolutely no such shipping movements at all. The fishing vessels at La Pallice commandeered by the Germans did not even open fire on them as they usually did. In confirmation of further orders, these aircraft then made an attack at 0930 on a German flak battery situated just north of the village of St. Pierre d'Oléron. The bombs were all direct hits and the results were very satisfactory. The enemy response to this attack was feeble and all the aircraft returned safely to base by 0950.[3]

> Later another division of six more SBDs from the 4th Flotilla was airborne, under the command of Lieutenant de Vaisseau Condroyer, and at 0900 had relieved the earlier patrol and maintained the continuing close watch over the harbour and sea.

They returned to base at 1230 having sighted nothing untoward. Cloud levels were lowering all the time, and visibility gradually closed down from 3,000 meters to 1,000 meters. No worthwhile objectives could be made out in this murk and eventually the aircraft jettisoned their bombs into the empty sea.

Between 1440 and 1600 Capitaine de Fregate Laine himself made a personal reconnaissance of the waters all around the Ile d'Oléron. There was no reaction to his very low-level snooping from the German flak batteries. The former French naval base on the island gave no appearance of having suffered any important damage despite the land fighting. Enemy resistance did not seem very lively either, nonetheless the French landing troops only appeared to be making much slow progress.[4]

Laine's account continued:

On 1 May, the division placed on the alert six more aircraft from 4 Flotille under the command of Lieutenant de Vaisseau Mellet and they were airborne at 0636. A French destroyer was said to be at anchor off the Pointe des Saumonards. This ship was not glimpsed. The ship was there to guide two transport ships from La Pallice to evacuate a party of German prisoners. The division therefore contented themselves with a bombing attack on German flak batteries at 3 Pierres (Ile d'Oléron) and achieved good results. Again there was no response from the enemy gunners and the aircraft landed back at 0800.[5]

This marked the end of the attacks on enemy positions on the island, for the German garrison surrendered in full two hours later on the same day. To prove that not all their work was so easy, a summary of the group's work in April 1945, was recorded by Laine with the following statistics:

Convoy Escort Sorties flown—177. Hours flown—277.
Reconnaissance Sorties flown—44. Hours flown—75.
Attack missions flown—444. Hours flown—624.
Tonnage of bombs dropped—246.[6]

Final close air support operations as the ring closed around Germany followed the same pattern on both the Western and Eastern fronts. Even at this stage of the war the Western and Soviet methods of control and direction of air strikes still lagged somewhat behind what the Luftwaffe had achieved at its peak in 1940–41. Thus, despite overwhelmingly superior numbers of all arms on both fronts, it still took the British, Americans, Canadians, and French twelve months from May 1944 to do what the Germans had done in a mere six weeks in 1940, and this with the bulk of the German forces holding back vastly superior numbers on the Eastern Front at the same time. Nonetheless the final outcome was as certain in Europe as it was in the Far East.

In the US Navy the Curtiss Helldiver was finally combat-tested when the VS and VB squadrons (Aircraft Scouting and Aircraft Bombing) were combined into one large unit as an experiment. This unit made its debut at Rabaul on 11 November 1943, led by navy pilot Bob Friesz. It was this same pilot who elaborated on what the main differences were between the army's feelings on dive-bombing and the navy's. These attitudes are important for they sum up why one service, be it the US Navy or the Luftwaffe, could make the dive-bomber and dive-bombing a brilliant success while another service (be it the USAAC or the RAF) just could not, or would not, make it work for them. Attitude.

> To be a good dive bomber pilot, you had to be firmly convinced that you were one. It's definitely hard on my pride to come back and say that I missed. Of course, a lot of us make sure of more hits by releasing very low. That prevents enemy surface craft from maneuvering to evade the bomb. It must be uppermost in your mind to get a hit whatever the cost may be or whatever the circumstances.
>
> When a Navy dive bomber speaks of releasing very low he means that he drops his bombs around 1,000 feet, or even lower. During World War II, the term dive bombing outside the US Navy has been used rather loosely to cover a variety of bombing operations. In the European and Mediterranean war theaters, land-based fighter planes were equipped with bomb racks, and in some cases dive flaps, and labelled as dive bombers. However, in normal operations, these fighter conversions released their bombs at 3,000 to 5,000 feet. Navy pilots who dropped at such high altitudes would undoubtedly be grounded by their commanders. Accuracy at that height could not be assured, even when using a true dive bomber.[7]

As we have seen, Friesz was unknowingly wronging many US Army A-36 pilots, who in combat pressed down as low as their navy counterparts, but overall his description was sound. It was not until the later

Against the difficult-to-spot and well-dug-in jungle targets presented by the Japanese in the South Pacific and in Burma, the Allies were forced to employ dive-bombing. The British, Australian, and Indian air forces in the Far East all employed the Vultee Vengeance dive-bomber in this very demanding duty during 1943–44, and it proved highly successful, especially at the battles of Imphal and Kohima. This photo shows three Vengeance aircraft of No. 82 Squadron, RAF, shortly after takeoff on a full-strength strike mission over a typical Burmese landscape. (D.V.S. Berrington)

Inset
Here, in a closer view, are three Vultee Vengeance dive-bombers of No. 12 Squadron, RAAF, which operated over the Timor Sea region in the 1943–44 period. (Australian War Memorial, Canberra ACT)

stages of the war with dive-bombing in France and Burma that the British, American army, and French land-based air forces began achieving results similar to those of the earlier German, Japanese, British Fleet Air Arm, and US Navy squadrons. According to another of the pilots from VB-17, "the more successful dive bomber pilots were those who were able to shake off thoughts of impending danger and got into action without misgivings."[8]

The only genuine dive-bomber to finally be used by the RAF was the Vultee Vengeance, which was used by four RAF and two Indian air force squadrons in Burma. Their accuracy was phenomenal and their work was highly praised. After the various Arakan campaigns the main role of these squadrons became holding off Japanese attacks against the surrounded garrisons at Kohima and Imphal in 1944. Here the Vengeance units were called upon to drop their bombs onto enemy positions that were within only a few feet from the defenders.

Although vital air support was flown by No. 20 Squadron with rocket-firing Hawker Hurricane IVs, Nos. 607 and 615 Squadrons with cannon-armed Hurricane Mark IICs, No. 27 Squadron with Bristol Beaufighters in the rocket and strafing role, and finally Curtiss Mohawks fitted to carry 20- or 30-pound armor-piercing incendiary bombs and 40-pound general purpose bombs, the Vengeance proved the only aircraft capable of pinpoint precision. The Vengeance could deliver a much heavier punch within a few feet of the target, usually in combinations of 500-pound, 250-pound, and incendiary bombs with varying time fuses.

A good cross-section of the dive-bombers' work was described by Lieutenant Colonel William H. Jones, representative of the Vultee company, in a report made in November 1943:

Now that the weather is permitting more activity, our dive bombers are the most popular with the advanced army units, operating against Japanese positions which have been prepared very thoroughly, and camouflaged in the usual expert way for which they are famous.

On 1 November General Sir Claude Auchinleck, Commander-in-Chief, India, made a tour of the Assam-Burma front. At one point in his tour of the Arakan sector he was within sight of the cleverly camouflaged Japanese positions. He had an excellent view of a Vengeance attack on enemy quarters and installations near Maungdaw, all the aircraft dropping their 500-pound bombs right in the target area and leaving several fires burning. So expert have these pilots become that the C-in-C was able to be very close to the targets hit and still be safe, to say nothing of the poor private, who is at best within a stone's throw to where the advanced enemy positions are being blasted. In other words one can always have a ring-side seat to the Vengeance at work.

Not many days back an advanced Army patrol discovered a Japanese strongpoint. Word was transmitted to their Commanding Officer, and he at once signalled, by radio, for six Vengeance dive bombers (this signal was direct to the Vengeance Squadron). Within forty-five minutes from the time the signal was made the first bombs burst on this position, and before the Vengeances had landed back at their base, word was received that "Target completely covered by your bombs, this point cleared of enemy opposition."

In discussing the work of the Vengeance dive bomber with a British Army Major, who had been in the forward positions relying on the support of our aircraft, he remarked that "Japanese troops have been continually bombed with uncomfortable accuracy by the Vengeance, which in thick jungle has proved an accurate and powerful weapon, we hope to see more of them as time goes by." One interesting comment from a pilot flying for the first time on an operational flight was "Our target was the jail at Akyab and as I dived down and released my bombs, I passed the jail going up!"

Reports that come to the Intelligence people of the RAF from enemy lines are very encouraging. Very seldom do we fail to have the enemy troop casualties listed, and, after one raid by six Vengeances, the report stated that fourteen truckloads of Japanese dead were removed from the area. In another case, several Japanese Officers had recovered a "time delay" bomb which had been dropped some six or seven hours previously. They, thinking it to be

The most accurate method of attacking well-concealed jungle targets, especially those that the Japanese so skillfully constructed within a few yards of Allied lines, was by precision dive-bombing. In Burma this task was fulfilled during 1943–44 by the Vultee Vengeance dive-bomber, which was operated by four squadrons of the RAF and two of the Indian air force. This photo shows the results of such attacks on a Japanese position in Burma by No. 110(H) Squadron, RAF.

The target is the village of Mutaik, which was bombed on 25 March 1944. It was a Japanese tank and motor transport repair center, situated east of the Chindwin River in a bend of a tributary. The precise target was the narrow end of the village, exactly covered in white smoke from incendiary bombs and the dark from high explosives. All bombs are on target. It will be noted from the tank tracks that since the bridge was not strong enough to carry such heavy vehicles, they left the road to drive through the river and rejoined the road on the other side. (Author's collection)

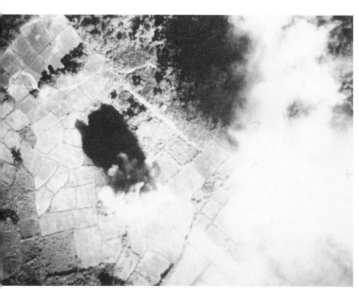

This photograph shows the village of Kuntawng bombed on 18 February 1944. It is on the edge of the jungle and mostly hidden by trees (as usual) with a cleared patch of paddy fields alongside. In this case the bombs were dropped by the Vultee Vengeance aircraft of No. 110(H) Squadron, RAF. (Author's collection)

a "dud," were getting very interested in the job of disassembling it when it went off in their faces. This one bomb accounted for twenty-four officers and men. And so continue the reports, all most favourably, and as the days pass with these reports coming along more and more people are looking to the Vengeance to be one of the major weapons used in the clearing of the Japanese out of the jungle and strongpoints they have established with so much hard work and cunning concealment.

One squadron for the month of October flew a total of 672 hours, and made a total of 546 sorties. During this period they maintained a record of 15 aircraft always serviceable out of 16.

Several Vengeance on this squadron have a total of near 250 hours time and using the words of their Engineering Officer, ". . . the airframe of these aircraft are in better shape than any I ever worked on." Major credit goes to this officer for the well-planned work and training of ground personnel in the proper maintenance of the Vengeance. He has recently retired from the ranks of the RAF, with twenty-four years service, all spent with aircraft, so he speaks with some degree of past experience on which to base his comments. With specific comments on maintenance, ". . . it's a piece of cake, if they want sixteen aircraft twice each day they can have them just as easy as twelve."[9]

In February 1944 the Japanese "Ha-Go" offensive was launched as a diversionary attack in Arakan. At the battle of Ngakyedauk Pass, to the east of Wabyin and the Naf River, the XV Corps of the British army was given continual close support from the air. Tactical bombing of the enemy was undertaken by two Vengeance squadrons which flew 269 sorties in just over one week while the Hurricanes hit at lines of communication, transport, and river and coastal transport, virtually bringing the Japanese attack to a halt.

In the critical battles for Nungshigum Hill in the spring of 1944, the Japanese gained the hillcrest on 11 April with artillery support and dug in. This was the closest the enemy got to Imphal itself. Two days later their positions were bombed and strafed for one and one half hours by the Vengeance dive-bombers and Hurricane fighter-bombers supported by artillery in a concerted plan. Then a fresh battalion of infantry went in supported by tanks.

Close support was given by both Hurricanes and Vengeances to IV and XXXIII Corps, which also struck Japanese forces on the roads and tracks behind the battle front at Kanglatongbi as well as supply and ammunition dumps in the Kabaw Valley in the area between Mintha and Kalewa. By 21 April the Vengeance squadrons had delivered 500 tons of bombs in 1,700 sorties in support of the troops on the ground.

In the resulting British double-envelopment battle by General Grover's forces on 25 April, the 4th and 5th Brigades moving up to the attack were supported by Vengeance sorties on a Naga village close to Kohima.

Perhaps the most outstanding victory achieved by the Tactical Air Force was during General Slim's audacious pincer attack on Meiktila in February 1945. In desperation the Japanese commander committed his only armored regiment in a counterattack against the 14th Army. The regiment moved by night and lay up in camouflaged revetments by day to avoid detection. But its ruse failed.

Packing the "Sunday Punch." Five-inch rockets proved very effective ground-support weapons, and not only in Europe. Here RAAF ground personnel load up a Bristol Beaufighter of No. 30 Squadron based at Noemfoor on 10 November 1944. The Beaufighter could carry eight of these weapons under its wings to attack "targets of opportunity," which included ships as well as land targets. (Australian War Memorial, Canberra ACT)

In the Southwest Pacific theater of war, the Royal Australian Air Force had by 1945 established powerful close air support units at Morotai. Here RAAF Bristol Beaufighters of No. 30 Squadron are seen deployed on the runway awaiting the call to action from the front-line troops. (Australian War Memorial, Canberra ACT)

On 19 February two Hawker Hurricanes sighted by chance a single tank in a gulley.

Attacking immediately, the pair set fire to the tank with their 40-mm cannon and then searched farther south. They found another tank in a chaung [gulley] 800 yards away. Relief for the Cab Rank patrol now arrived and more Hurricanes were summoned, some with cannon and some with rockets. In all during the day, thirteen tanks were discovered and all were destroyed. The enemy had complete confidence in his camouflage, offering no resistance in protection of what was in fact the heaviest concentration of enemy armor found in the Burma War. This absence of defense removed the need for any evasive action, and the pilots were able to concentrate on searching. They found that most often one or two shells were enough to set fire to the tanks, which normally burned lightly for a few minutes and then burst into a good blaze which lasted about an hour.[10]

Against the forty-five-foot-thick walls of Fort Dufferin a "master bomber" technique was employed by Group Captain B. A. Chacksfield, OBE. He crisscrossed the sky over the disputed citadel and directed his attack wing by radio. Assaults were made by bomb-carrying Thunderbolts and Hurricanes supported by American B-25s.

Chacksfield later recalled: "He [the master bomber] watched the bombs of the first aircraft hit the upward-sloping earth ramparts and skip over the walls out of the fort before exploding. So he switched the attack round, bombing from the outside in. The master bomber advised, too, on the run, height and precise spot at which to keep hammering. By the efforts of all the bombers twenty-six separate gaps were made in the great walls."[11]

Undoubtedly Britain's premier World War II RAF dive-bomber pilot was Arthur Murland Gill. Not only did he almost single-handedly, and with great determination, build up No. 84 RAF Vengeance squadron in India despite official indifference and the many mechanical problems encountered but his inspired and determined style of leading from the front endeared him to his squadron in a manner that still evokes fond memories more than forty years later. More, he brought the operational usage of the dive-bomber to prominence; the expertise and skill of No. 84 Squadron became a byword in Burma, bringing very high commendation from Mountbatten, Wingate, and other senior officers.

When the Japanese war began, No. 84 was one of several Blenheim squadrons rushed eastward and Gill recalled their long journey in January 1942, in which they flew out to Sumatra just three weeks before Singapore fell. The squadron was caught up in this debacle and suffered heavy losses; only eight of the twenty-four Blenheim IVLs survived to fly to new bases in Java. By March the 136 survivors from an original strength of 605 officers and men reached Karachi, among them Arthur Gill. A score of others survived an epic boat voyage to reach Australia but most of the others passed into the hell of Japanese POW camps.

Eighty-four Squadron was decimated and threatened with disbandment. Only the iron determination and persistence of Arthur Gill kept the unit in existence during this harsh period. He campaigned ceaselessly to have the squadron reequipped instead and, to his lasting credit, won his case. 84 Squadron was one of four (the others being 45, 82, 84 and 110 Squadrons) selected to convert to the new Vultee Vengeance dive-bomber then being shipped from America. Two squadrons of the Indian air force, 7 and 8, were also equipped with this aircraft and these six squadrons conducted a whole series of highly successful army cooperation missions during the years 1942–44. Although almost wholly ignored by official historians, these squadrons were nonetheless much praised at the time by the men on the ground, who only saw the results

The continued growth of the close-support low-level strafing aircraft, as envisaged prewar by the USAC, reached its ultimate development and size in the North American B-25 Mitchell bomber. This version carried a mighty punch, with a 75-mm cannon and two 50-caliber machine guns in its all-metal nose. This cannon, the largest mounted in a ground-support aircraft up to that date, could punch holes in warship hulls as well as knock out tanks, but the aircraft itself was large and unwieldy compared to the single-engine equivalents operating in the air forces of Germany and Britain at this period. (Official US Air Force photo, Washington, DC)

of their work and knew nothing of the enormous prejudice that they had to overcome from their own air marshals to be able to operate dive-bombers at all!

Steadily the squadron was rebuilt with Arthur Gill working tirelessly to assemble the new aircraft and draft and experiment using new tactics with little or no guidance and certainly no encouragement. He not only had to start from scratch and make his men live and breathe dive-bombing but he had to ensure that their new-found skills were properly utilized by men who knew nothing about the method and cared less. He managed to do all these things.

Holding together and then revitalizing 84 Squadron was Arthur Gill's biggest achievement. In the course of extensive interviews at his home Gill was generous in his memories of this period. His recall of details and his vast collection of photographs and documents provided a real treasure-trove of facts about these units.

The OC No. 168 Wing and station commander at Kumbhirgram was Group Captain E. A. Whiteley (nicknamed "Titch" Whiteley because he was small). Although OC, he never flew Vengeances or flew with us. I normally flew as Wing Leader whenever more than one Vengeance squadron operated together on a maximum effort attack. In all I led 1,476 operational sorties against Japanese HQ, troops, supplies, ammunition dumps, tanks, AFVs, rail and road communications, bridges, and airfields in support of General Wingate's Long-Range Penetration Group (the 3d Indian Division) and the 14th Army. The reason I was chosen by OC 168 Wing and HQ 221 Group to act as the wing leader was because I always had the good fortune to find the target without exception, which wasn't always easy.

I had seven nationalities on the squadron—counting English, Irish, Scots and Welsh as one; namely British, Australian, New Zealanders, Rhodesians, Canadians, an American, and a French-Canadian. The one American pilot, "Curly" Keech, was killed

during a raid which I led when he was hit by ground fire during the dive and crashed in the target area.[12]

Two often-perpetuated and seemingly self-sustaining myths Arthur Gill firmly demolished were first, that the Vengeance squadrons in Burma did not conduct true vertical dive-bombing but made shallow angle attacks and second, that they flew only with fighter cover. Both, he later wrote, were complete untruths.

> I think that dive-bombing at anything under an angle of about 80 degrees is a complete waste of time. You can't push over, you can't see over your nose. One might have got away with it in things like Beaufighters where you had the engines stuck out ahead of the nose and where you could see forward in a shallow dive. But where you've got a thumping great engine and no view forward, unless you get right on top of your target you're not going to see anything. And if you came down like that, in a shallow attack, the bombs are going to land miles short. We always, with a very few exceptions later in the monsoon season, went in vertically on our targets.
>
> As for fighter cover, we rarely had it. About 95 percent of our bombing missions in Burma were made with no fighter escort whatsoever. For a start they had not the range to accompany us all the way. Looking at my flying log book I can see we had fighters with us on one or two occasions earlier on, and that was it.[13]

Gill worked very closely with General Wingate when he was planning what proved to be his last Chindit raid behind enemy lines. He wanted very close air support to be on call and he came and watched the young Vengeance crews practicing with his troops beforehand. He said little but afterward he grilled Gill intensively until he got all the answers.

Nothing was said at the time but in October 1943 Lord Louis Mountbatten wrote to Gill confirming that 84 Squadron was the one Wingate wanted to back him and that he had been clearly impressed at their accuracy. As it turned out, calls for similar support for the besieged British troops at Kohima and Imphal occupied 84 Squadron and it was not able to help Wingate as much as it would have liked to.

After the Japanese attacks had been beaten off by air power, the Allies took the offensive. Gill described the Vengeance attack formations in this manner: "We normally flew in groups of twelve aircraft, in boxes of four with boxes stepped down. The sixth and twelfth aircraft would carry cameras. As they approached the target they would switch on the cameras, then bomb doors open, dive brakes out, those on the Vengeance opened both below and above the wing simultaneously for steadiness. We often dropped delay-action bombs when attacking bridge and rail targets."[14]

The last Vengeance combat mission of the war was led by Arthur Gill on 16 July 1944, when twelve aircraft hit Japanese ammunition dumps at Le-U.

By 1945 the Vengeance squadrons had been reequipped with DeHavilland Mosquito twin-engine bombers. These were fast and could carry enormous bomb loads. They had been a great success in Europe. They were built of wood and used a special glue to hold them together. When first employed in the heat of the East this glue was not always satisfactory, and there were reports of wings falling off. The Vengeance was slow but built like a tank of all-metal construction. More important, it did the precise job the army required—it placed its bombs directly on target with consistency and accuracy. Regardless, progress must have its day and they disappeared. More useful was the arrival of Bristol Beaufighters, another twin-engine machine with a good cannon armament. The low-level strikes conducted by these machines soon earned them the nickname "Whispering Death" among the Japanese soldiers. Even Supermarine Spitfires of the RAF and the Indian air force conducted dive-bombing and ground-strafing missions toward the end of the campaign with great success.

In the north of Burma the various American contingents fighting with Stilwell's forces had utilized both the A-36 Invaders and the P-51 Mustangs in ground-support missions from 1943 onward. Some of these machines were fitted with bazooka rocket launchers but mainly it was with bombs and their guns that they carried out their missions. In China proper the original American Volunteer Group, with their P-40Es, was merged into regular army air force units in July 1942, and these were expanded as the war continued. They also conducted both dive-bomber and strafing missions at infrequent intervals, but finally their bases were overrun in the Japanese offensive launched to clear the land route to Thailand and Burma, which the fighter-bombers proved powerless to halt.

In the southwest Pacific the bulk of the land fighting was taking place in New Guinea, where General Kenney was using all manner of aircraft to give the army aerial firepower. A whole wing of Royal Australian Air Force Vultee Vengeance dive-bombers operated for six weeks from Nadzab and were most valued. A political decision removed them but the RAAF continued to fly close-support missions with Curtiss Kittyhawks, although with less accuracy and a higher casualty rate as these fighters were not so robust on the jungle airstrips as the Vengeances had been.

The RAAF also used Commonwealth Boomerang and Wirraways as accurate "target markers" with smoke bombs to indicate jungle targets. From September 1944 to May 1945 Australian Beauforts and Boomerangs of No. 71 Wing flew hundreds of sorties each month in the Aitape-Wewak area, most in the direct-support role for ground operations by the 6th Division. In the later stages of this campaign, bomb-carrying RNZAF Chance Vought Corsairs based at Torokina were led to the targets by Boomerangs and Australian Bristol Beaufighters and took a heavy toll.

The Pacific island-hopping war had meanwhile worked its way, island by island, up the Solomons chain toward Rabaul in New Britain. Although the bulk of the close air support work was again conducted by the US Marine Corps dive-bombers, the Royal New Zealand Air Force established No. 25 Squadron, with Douglas SBD-5 dive-bombers, and it flew into Piva airstrip on Bougainville island in March 1944. Here it flew combat missions against Japanese artillery positions that were actually shelling the airstrip as the planes took off. Close support indeed.

When the Americans got ashore once more in the Philippines, close air support was provided by a specially set up and highly trained United States Marine Corps wing, equipped with Douglas SBD-5 dive-bombers and a comprehensive radio net, mobile and finely tuned. Intensive study was made into providing reliable and accurate air attack for the army and it was a great disappointment to the Marine airmen when they found themselves underemployed in their ground-attack role in the subsequent fighting.

The island campaigns eventually culminated at Okinawa and Iwo Jima and here fanatical Japanese resistance called for the best of close-support operations by US Navy and Marine Corps flyers. They mainly used the big and powerful Chance Vought F4U Corsair fighter in this

Another form of close air support was the dropping of essential supplies and ammunition to front-line troops in difficult terrain. On both the Russian front in Europe and in the jungles of Papua, New Guinea, the versatility of the close-support aircraft enabled equipment to be pinpoint-dropped to the men on the ground. Here a canister is being loaded under the wing of an RAAF Wirraway for one such supply mission. (Australian War Memorial, Canberra ACT)

Like the United States Marine Corps, the Royal Navy's Fleet Air Arm deployed in large numbers aboard the six aircraft carriers of the British Pacific Fleet (Task Force 57) soon found out that the powerful Chance Vought F4U Corsair fighter-bomber could lift a greater bomb load than equivalent dive-bombers like the SBD. Because of the lack of aerial opposition, the British fliers soon imitated the Marine Corps in deploying this big machine as a ground-support aircraft, especially in the Okinawa campaign of 1945. (Fleet Air Arm Museum, Yeovilton)

role. It could carry twice the bomb load of a Dauntless as well as lethal combinations of rockets, napalm, and cannon. It proved highly versatile and rugged in both operations. On Iwo the enemy were dug in and concealed in caves only yards away from the runways the Corsairs were operating from, so they were bombing without even retracting their undercarriages.

The bulk of the Japanese army close-support aircraft were held in readiness with the Kwantung Army on the Manchurian borders. Here the old Kawasaki Ki-48 light bombers were still equipping the bulk of the direct-support squadrons and were clearly no match for the highly proficient Soviet ground-attack forces honed to perfection against a far stronger opponent. In all some six hundred bombers were available to the Japanese, but only a third were of the close-support type.

The Soviets' main achievement was the transportation eastward, in double-quick time, of enormous masses of men and machines designed to crush the Japanese forces. By the eve of the attack 7 August 1945, no less than 479 ground-attack planes were in place, along with 1,573 fighters, 740 bombers, and 153 reconnaissance aircraft. The attack squadrons' orders were to support the ground troops as they broke through the Japanese fortified frontier regions, to operate against staff headquarters and communications centers to destroy control, and to break any concentrations that sought to make a stand.

As part of the intensive preparations beforehand, the ground-attack units practiced techniques of hitting small targets like pillboxes. A series

The last island to fall to the Americans in World War II was Iwo Jima. The Japanese defenders fought with their usual fanatical courage and were hard to destroy in their networks of caves and gun pits. Napalm was one way of smoking out these hidden nests. Here a US Marine Corps Chance Vought F4U Corsair (center top of photo), operating from an airstrip within a few hundred yards of the enemy, deposits its load of flaming jelly on one such enemy concentration. (Official US Marine Corps photo, Washington, DC)

of control-recognition signs were placed along the border and on major roads, and radio-directing equipment, lights, and signals were organized. These communications units moved up to the forward air bases prior to the attack. This all helped to improve Soviet ground control over its attack aircraft. Air technical groups were set up to liaise with the air regiments. Plans were made to use troops and army engineering units to build additional airstrips.

The results were the greatest vindication yet of Soviet direct-support methods. Everywhere the attack swept forward, overrunning and swamping the Japanese fortifications. Typical of the many actions was that carried out by the Pe.2 dive-bombers of the 34th Bomber Air Division under Colonel K. A. Mikhakylov against frenzied Japanese defenses in the Khutou area. A strike of eighty-one aircraft was thrown at this resistance. The official Soviet history records that: "They struck at targets within the fortified region, destroyed a series of pillboxes, and silenced the Japanese mortar and artillery fire. Taking advantage of enemy confusion, Soviet troops broke through to the fortified region, and two days later, captured it." [15]

At the battle of Mutanchiag on 16 August, the Japanese launched a powerful counterattack. This was met by the aircraft of 252d Ground Attack Air Division under Lieutenant Colonel V. K. Makarov. According to official Soviet historians: "They attacked in waves against artillery, tanks, and infantry in support of our troops. Due to the joint efforts of our ground and air forces, the enemy was decisively defeated in the Mudantszyan district." [16]

It was much the same story in the Dunin fortified region. Nineteen Bomber Air Corps sent in 108 aircraft against this target. Again, from the official Soviet account: "The effect of this action was very great. After the areas had been occupied, it was established that direct hits from large bombs had destroyed four pillboxes, two bunkers, a munitions dump, killed 130 men and wounded many soldiers and officers." [17]

One of the last attacks in this brief and decisive campaign was made on 12 August 1945 by Il-2s led by Lieutenant Colonel I. A. Kochergin. The Soviet air force history claimed: "Our fliers made as many as five passes at the target and compelled the enemy to cease his fire. The Japanese soldiers sustained great losses, raised a white flag, and surrendered." [18]

In Kwantung, as elsewhere in the Far East, it was all over by 15 August. Thus ended World War II, with direct air support held in high regard.

seven

Reduction and
Revival

In the immediate postwar era came another false dawn of a
lasting peace on earth. With the three Axis powers totally
defeated, the two western Allies commenced wholesale dis-
armament. The wartime alliance did not long survive the
peace, and the Soviet Union, far from disarming, promoted
the spread of the Communist creed the whole globe over. In Great Britain
the armed forces were cut back to the bone until, by 1948, they were
barely adequate even for colonial policing. The Communist insurgency
first hit the British in Malaya and search-and-destroy missions in the
heavy jungle of the interior called for air support of the patrols.

To conduct close-support missions the RAF introduced a new twin-
engine light bomber, the Bristol Brigand. This machine had originally
been conceived as a torpedo bomber during the war but the Air Staff
revised the specification to that of a light ground-attack bomber and as
such it became the last piston-engine bomber to serve in the RAF. This
midwing three-seater had a useful gun armament of four 20-mm cannon
clustered in the nose in a manner similar to the American prewar attack
aircraft. It had wing racks for up to 2,000 pounds of bombs, or alter-
nately it could carry a large complement of 3-inch rockets for striking
ground targets. It had a maximum speed of 358 mph and as it was des-
tined for overseas squadrons, the Brigand was fully tropicalized.

Although only 143 were ever built under the financial stringency of
the times, they proved good value. All in all the Brigand was to prove the
ideal craft for the role into which it was thrust, first in Iraq, then in

Postwar, the tradition of using navy attack aircraft from their secure aircraft carrier bases out at sea to attack guerrilla forces inland in support of their own troops was taken up by the French in Indochina (Vietnam, Laos, and Cambodia) during their initial struggle with the Vietminh Communist forces in the Red River area. Here a Douglas SBD-5 Dauntless prepares to take off from the French aircraft carrier *Dixmude* to undertake such a strike. (ECP Armées, Fort D'Ivry)

The French navy also employed refurbished Curtiss SB2C Helldivers purchased from the US aboard the light carrier *Arromanches* in the Gulf of Tonkin, striking at targets deep inside the Communist-held delta around Hanoi. Here, Lieutenant Commander H. de Lestapis (kneeling on the left) and his air and ground crew of the French navy's 3 Flotille prepare the flight logbooks before commencing another such mission in 1952. (Captain H. de Lestapis)

Aden, and finally in its major combat role with No. 45 Squadron in Malaya. Between 1950 and 1954 the Brigands of this squadron were continually in action against guerrilla bands flushed out by the army and Royal Marines. Attacks were conducted at low level with all weapons—cannon, bombs, and rockets—and proved particularly effective.

Of course, not only the British had postwar problems in their colonial empire. The Dutch were strongly resisted when they reoccupied their former empire of Java and Sumatra. Fierce nationalist opposition was encountered as early as 1945 and a very bloody campaign was fought, with British help, before they could reestablish themselves.

Likewise the French found the Communist Vietminh waiting for them when they reoccupied Indochina. A long and protracted war began in 1946 and continued without letup for another ten years until the French, isolated and unsupported by their western partners, gave up the struggle. As with most guerrilla campaigns, the combat gradually escalated into a full-scale war.

Initially the French navy had sent its old SBD Dauntless squadrons out to the Far East on carriers and they held the line with air strikes against the Communists whenever they broke cover and engaged in pitched battles. This resulted in several repulses for the Vietminh and so they reverted to guerrilla tactics for a while. Then the French forced a final showdown battle in which they expected their close-support air power to prove their key to victory.

At the decisive battle of Dien Bien Phu No. 3 Carrier Assault Flotilla's SB-C2 Helldivers, commanded by Lieutenant Andrieux and embarked aboard the aircraft carrier *Arromanches* (under Captain A. Patou), provided the spearhead of meaningful close air support until 30 April 1954. These dive-bombers were supplemented by the Grumman F6F Hellcat fighters of 11 Carrier Fighter Flotilla acting in the fighter-bomber role from the same ship. They initially supplemented the Grumman F8F Bearcat fighter-bombers of the French air force's 1/22 "Saintonge" and 2/22 "Languedoc" fighter groups until these were decimated by the Vietminh artillery fire on the besieged airstrip. The dive-bombers also received support from the navy's 28 Bomber Flotilla equipped with PB4Y2 Privateers and the air force's B-26 Marauders of 1/25 Tunisie. All attacks in support of the base were coordinated by Lieutenant Colonel Dossol's Bombardment Subgroup.

The role of the air forces in the operation was, of course, crucial, both in basic supply and support. It had been spelled out in a communication sent by General Henri Navaree to Brigadier General Rene Cogny on 3 December 1953. This read: "The mission of the air force shall be, until further orders, to give priority and with the maximum means at its disposal, to the support of our forces in the North-West. The Commanding General of the air force in the Far East will, to that effect, reinforce the Northern Tactical Air Group."[1]

What the order ignored was the inability of the severely limited forces at the disposal of the French air force and navy to provide such support in anything like the numbers required. This was due to the basic miscalculation of the French upper command in Hanoi, which sealed the fate of the whole campaign, as to the scale and vigor of the Vietminh response and their ability to transport heavy equipment and large numbers of combat divisions by manpower to the scene of the battle. Dien Bien Phu was a mousetrap set by the French to deliberately entice a stand-up battle. Unfortunately for the French they succeeded only too well and ended up not with a mouse but with a tiger! This underestimation of the enemy, the cardinal sin of warfare, was deep-rooted in the French army in Indochina. For example Colonel Charles Piroth proclaimed shortly before the battle that "Firstly, the Vietminh won't succeed in getting their artillery through to here. Secondly, if they do get here, we'll smash them. Thirdly, even if they manage to keep on shooting, they will be unable to supply their pieces with enough ammunition to do us any real harm."[2]

Every one of these prophecies proved incorrect, and in March the poor, disillusioned colonel, his own guns smashed or overrun, pulled a grenade on himself as acceptance of blame for his misplaced optimism. So it was on air support that the garrison depended more and more as the siege progressed. The supporting aircraft were just too few to make up for the four-to-one superiority the Vietminh managed to achieve in heavy artillery, especially as their guns were concealed in firing pits with only their muzzles protruding. The French guns, by contrast, were out in the open in a severely restricted space and easily located.

Moreover, the much-heralded Operation "Strangle" conducted by the United States air force to cut similar two-legged supply lines in Korea during 1951–52 had ended in total failure to limit enemy supplies. In the jungle-covered hills of North Vietnam the supply routes and roads were even more difficult to spot, let alone destroy, even if the French could have matched US airborne firepower. But of course they didn't have a fraction of it. Vietminh General Giap was to boast, "Our soldiers knew well the art of camouflage, and we succeeded in getting our supplies through."[3] This art of camouflage extended to tying together the tops of tall trees to form an archway of leaves to conceal their movements even by day. Special emphasis was always placed by the Communists on concealment from the air. It became the duty of every Vietminh soldier when on the march to carry on his shoulders a kind of framework which was covered with leaves and foliage by the man marching behind. As the area of the jungle changed, so the vegetation of the camouflage was altered to suit and blend in perfectly. The biggest asset the Communists had was of course their endless supply of manpower, the impressed peasants of the *da cong*, whom they used ruthlessly and with complete indifference for individual loss or injury.

Thus the French flew many interdiction missions between November 1953 and May 1954 to cut the vital supply links of Roads 13B and 41B leading up from the Red River and across the Black River toward Dien Bien Phu. Although a heavy toll of the enemy was taken, the Communist buildup never slackened. The air over the fortress itself was a maze of flak, but the approach routes were almost as comprehensively protected. In December, for example, during the course of 367 combat sorties, 49 French aircraft received damaging hits. This led to a diversion of dive-bomber attacks away from supporting the paratroopers or cutting enemy supply lines and into pure antiflak suppression sorties, all of which suited Giap's buildup plans admirably.

Much of the French navy dive-bombers' work was intervention, or cutting the vital roads leading into Dien Bien Phu down which so much material and manpower was laboriously being built up. On 5 January, for example, a strike was launched against the vital road junction town of Conoi (codenamed "Jezabel"), where the main highways of Roads 41 and 13B met and became Road 41B, the final artery of the Vietminh buildup. At 1230 nine Helldivers were sent to attack this point, each aircraft armed with 500- and 1,000-pound bombs. The weather at sea and over the target was perfect and clear, and very accurate attacks were made on Conoi itself. Strafing attacks were also made on the return journey at Thai Binh and Tutien where camouflaged vehicles were located and burnt.

Similar missions continued. On 7 January one typical sortie was flown against position "Melchior," farther along Road 41B, east of Tuan Giao. Nine Helldivers dropped a variety of bombs on this position, four of them 1,000-pound weapons with delay-action fuses of twelve and twenty-four hours to remain effective and cause maximum disruption over a long period. They also dropped six M.131 "Butterfly" bombs.

Periodically the *Arromanches* had to leave her station and steam north to Hong Kong to replenish, since the French had virtually no ships capable of underway replenishment at this time. During such absences it became practice for sections of the dive-bomber unit to fly ashore and continue operations from land bases, the principal one being Bach Mai near Hanoi itself. It was from here on 19 January for example that six Helldivers operated against enemy-held positions near Nha Trang in conjunction with Operation "Arethusa," a suboperation of the main French offensive, which was codenamed "Atlante."

But as the Vietminh closed in more and more, so the dive-bombers found themselves bombing targets much closer to the besieged garrison itself. On 29 January ten SBC-2C-5s took off between 1330 and 1415 hours to bomb and strafe the area just eight kilometers north-northeast of Dien Bien Phu. Bad weather over the target area negated much of their accuracy on this mission, although twenty 1,000-pound and ten 500-pound bombs were planted in the target area and strafing was conducted on positions fifteen kilometers southwest of the garrison. The results could not be observed by the crews.

All the time, the enemy was sapping closer and closer. On 3 February a typical mission involved eight Helldivers who hit dug-in enemy positions six kilometers east of the main French defenses with twelve out of sixteen 1,000-pound bombs and six out of eight 500-pounders, while also strafing the target. Two of the aircraft aborted but delivered their bombs on enemy positions at Thai Binh instead. That January, 3F had dropped 436 1,000-pound and 358 500-pound bombs on the enemy as well as 51 "Butterfly" bombs, 38 loads of napalm, and 15,000 rounds of machine-gun fire.

The same heavy work load continued during February 1954. On 2 February for instance, an attack was made on thick plantations some fifteen kilometers north-northeast of Dien Bien Phu which were thought to conceal an artillery ammunition dump. Five Helldivers made accurate attacks and planted eight bombs on this target and on Hill 41, which was used as an observation position for the Vietminh gunners. Both targets were hard hit and a large column of white smoke indicated that at least one supply dump had been blown up. The only losses up to 11 February were two SBCs damaged by accidents during landings. On 8 February Helldiver 89.367 missed a wire landing on the carrier and went into the crash barrier, which necessitated a new engine and prop. But these were normal working hazards of carrier operations. Immunity over the target was, however, soon to become a thing of the past as the number of antiaircraft guns deployed by Giap's forces steadily increased.

Arromanches had to return to Hong Kong between 15 and 23 February and once more a detachment of six Helldivers worked from Bach Mai while the Hellcats operated out of Cat Bi field near Haiphong. Those aircraft that remained aboard the carrier were rotated to give all flying personnel a break from what was becoming an increasingly wearing and hazardous nonstop period of combat flying. The sortie rate of the dive-bombers ashore in no way lessened, ranging from between eight and twelve sorties per day except for one day, 23 February, when the weather prevented most flying.

124

In the aftermath of World War II the French also relied initially on American aircraft to equip their forces until their own aircraft industry recovered and produced its own types. Here are four Republic F84F Thunderstreak jets with long-range fuel tanks. They were employed in the ground-attack role for use against potential Russian aggression in Europe, when France was still a full member of the NATO alliance. (SHAA, Paris)

The carrier returned to her flying-off position and the pounding continued unabated. In one attack on 1 March, five Helldivers dropped eight 260-pound bombs on enemy positions in the region thirty kilometers northeast of Dien Bien Phu itself. The army observation posts later signaled back that the attackers' accuracy was "excellent." The outward leg was flown at 7,000 feet and they returned at 11,000 feet to miss the worst of the flak concentrations.

It was a different story on 13 March. Two strikes were made by the SBCs this day. Launchings took place between 1530 and 1600 respectively. The first attack was carried out by four aircraft, which hit artillery positions a bare six kilometers east of Dien Bien Phu with four 500-pound bombs. Explosions on target were observed. The second mission was conducted by five additional Helldivers against enemy guns located six kilometers northeast and six kilometers south of the two extremities of the French fortress, now itself under a veritable hail of explosive shell. Ten 1,000-pound and fourteen 500-pound bombs were delivered against these artillery positions in an effort to relieve the pounding the trapped French paratroops were undergoing, but detailed observations could not be made. The reason was the same for both missions, "reaction violente de la DCA sur l'objectif."[4] Why was the flak so intense? The main Vietminh assault was under way.

Just before the main Communist assault commenced on 13 March, General Henri Charles Lauzin, the French Commander, sent a telegram demanding that all the ground-support pilots should take "exceptional risks" in support of their brothers on the ground. This exhortation the navy dive-bomber pilots would follow to the letter and at considerable cost to themselves.

Although the main battle has often been compared to Verdun in the First World War or Stalingrad, Bataan, Corregidor, Tobruk, and L'Orient in the Second, as far as close air support involvment and the nature of the terrain were concerned, it much more resembled Kohima and Imphal in the Burma campaign of 1944. Unfortunately for the French, their forces both on the ground and in the air were smaller by far than those deployed by the Allies in those world war battles. Moreover, France's isolation was more complete, both in distance and ease of access. The Vietminh were similar to the Japanese in their tenacity, fanaticism, and methods of siege warfare. Both the Vietnamese and the Japanese were experts in jungle concealment and in trench warfare of great sophistication.

However, General Vo Nguyen Giap's Vietminh regiments had the incalculable advantage of large numbers of modern antiaircraft weapons, especially the superb Russian-built, Chinese-supplied and -manned 37-mm weapons, guns that could reach up to 8,500 feet and were sited in an ever-tightening ring on the hills overlooking the French base. Indeed, before the siege had been underway many days, some enemy flak gunners were depressing the muzzles of their weapons and firing *down* on the transport and ambulance aircraft running the gauntlet. The termination of hostilities in Korea at this time released ample numbers of such weapons and Red China made no bones about supplying both them and the skilled gunners to use them.

By March, for instance, a complete and fully equipped Chinese antiaircraft regiment, with sixty-four 37-mm guns, had arrived at Dien Bien Phu and was quickly emplaced. They reinforced about a score of such guns already in place there. With these weapons manned almost exclusively by the Chinese themselves it was in fact a Red Chinese unit, although a few Vietminh officers and men were added to give it "respectability" to the many naive and complaisant Western journalists reporting the war. Each of the sixty-four guns was dispersed singly around the perimeter so that the presence of the Chinese was heavily diluted among the other Communist forces there. They would ultimately claim to have hit sixty-two French aircraft during the course of the battle, almost one apiece.

Their sites did not remain static but were continually moved so they could not be pinned down by counterstrike dive-bombing attack. This effectively counteracted the French policy of "saturation" attacks in which twelve to fourteen aircraft would concentrate their dives on particular target areas where it was estimated enemy guns were massed. This game of blindman's bluff was easily won by the Vietminh, and even the liberal use of napalm had little effect on the sodden and soaked jungle once the rainy season had set in.

The amount of ordnance that jet fighter-bombers could haul into combat steadily increased as their power plants grew more and more efficient. Here a French air force pilot displays the hardware his mount could deliver, including 500- and 250-pound bombs, rockets, and napalm. (SHAA, Paris)

Preparing for takeoff against the Vietminh guerrillas in the jungles of Indochina is a French air force F8F Bearcat fighter-bomber. The payload includes both rockets and 250-pound bombs. It is interesting to note that the chalked markings on the bombs are almost identical to those carried by the German Stukas in their missions against Poland in September 1939. (SHAA, Paris)

The location of the fighting worked against the French from the very start. Situated in a valley at the far northwest end of the country, close to the Laotian border, it was at the maximum range of the single-engine dive-bombers and fighter-bombers flying from the *Arromanches*, which reduced the time they could spend over the target, even without heavy flak. Thus they could not linger over the battle zone to the same extent as the American A-1 Skyraiders were able to later in that area. The distance to be traveled and the need to conserve fuel also restricted their choice of approaches to the target, which in turn further assisted the Red gunlayers in predicting their approach course.

Undaunted, nine Helldivers carried out an attack on 14 March against artillery positions east of the fortress and dropped twenty-eight 260-pound and five 250-pound bombs. They also contributed twenty-four 5-inch rockets and ten antipersonnel clusters to the discomfort of the Vietminh. They claimed to have damaged one major enemy battery by direct hits. Again they reported fierce counterfire from both 12.7- and 37-mm flak guns. Two Helldivers were hit and damaged at this time, but both made it back to base and were quickly repaired and returned to battle.

On 15 March came the fall of the first of the strong outlying French fortresses. Well garrisoned with seasoned troops, bristling with artillery and mortars, Hill "Gabrielle" had faced the enemy full of confidence. But after the devastating artillery bombardment that pulverized its defenses, it was quickly overrun by massed "human-wave" infantry assaults. It fell in a breathlessly short time with heavy casualties. The navy fliers did all they could to assist the defenders, in spite of the fact that the valley was closed down with low clouds which reduced visibility enormously.

Four sorties were flown on this crucial day by the SBCs. In the first—the only one to reach the target due to the weather conditions—four Helldivers braved the crescendo of flak to strike at artillery pieces eight kilometers from the fortress, hitting them with four 500-pound bombs and sixteen 5-inch rockets, but they could not see the results due to the heavy antiaircraft fire. Four 1,000-pound bombs were put on target close by Gabrielle itself. Two more dive-bombers had their mission aborted by weather conditions but put their 1,000-pound bombs on targets in the Son-La region instead. The same fate befell others: One pair delivered eight 500-pound bombs and eight rockets on enemy emplacements twenty-five kilometers east of the basin and another pair bombed Gia-phu instead.

In addition to the navy dive-bombers, two of the few surviving Bearcats got airborne but one was destroyed. A bold dive-bombing attack by 11Fs Hellcat fighters, each carrying a single 500-pound bomb, resulted in the destruction by flak of Lieutenant Lestapis's aircraft.

The weather eased up on 31 March allowing the air force Bearcats and navy Helldivers to renew their close-support missions in strength. Their main sortie was to help the French counterattack regain three of their defense positions east of the main fortress, D2, E1, and E2, which had been overrun by the enemy the preceding day.

These bloody attacks resulted in the greatest victories achieved by the French during the battle. Despite the huge flak barrage, the Helldiver pilots did their utmost to help their comrades below. As in many instances during World War II, it was widely stated by the ground troops that the navy dive-bomber pilots pressed in much closer to carry out their attacks than did their air force colleagues. It was not a matter of courage but of training. Indeed, Bernard Fall was to state that the *Arromanches* SB-2C pilots "were loved by the paratroops for the risks they took, and for which they paid a higher price in lives than the Air Force."[5]

On this day of victory, when the Vietminh were swept back off all three positions and retreated with heavy losses, the cost to 3-F was high, for it was the Helldiver of Lieutenant Jean Dominique Andrieux, with his navigator/gunner Petty Officer 2d Class Jannie, that became enmeshed in the deadly web of flak from pumping 37-mms over strongpoint "Beatrice." Their aircraft disintegrated and both were killed. It was a heavy blow. It was the only loss from seventeen sorties flown by the Helldivers that day. Andrieux's place as commander of the dive-bomber squadron was taken by Lieutenant de Vaisseau de Lestapis and the missions continued.

Some observers have pointed out that the French contributed in some way to the incredible accuracy of the Vietminh flak gunners. They claim that French radio security was incredibly lax. For example, Charles Favrel reported on a supply-drop mission with which he flew. He was amazed, his article in *Le Monde* read, when he heard, ". . . transmitted in the clear, messages and orders to aircraft arriving on bombing missions or bringing in reinforcements or material!"[6] Broadcasting such information enabled guns to be laid in easy anticipation of each incoming French flight. But even without such slackness, the limited and ever-shrinking perimeter ruled out much in the way of diversion over the target once the planes were committed to their attack approaches.

The French navy Helldivers continued their operations. The improved weather conditions on 1 April enabled combat sorties to be increased to ninety-nine which helped stabilize the newly won front line and raised the defenders' morale considerably.

It needed raising. The constant enemy heavy artillery bombardment was rapidly reducing the French ability to reply in kind and, by 2 April, so great a loss had been taken by the French gunners that it was directed that all counterbattery work would in future have to be undertaken by the dive-bombers alone in the area facing fortress Beatrice. Only twelve French heavy guns remained in service at this point, and even this level was not to be maintained for very much longer. Bombs and napalm rained down on the last remnants of the Vietminh regiments holding positions on the flanks of the retaken positions, but French losses had also been heavy. Their casualties could not be replaced except by small numbers parachuted in, whereas fresh Communist regiments were arriving all the time. The enemy artillery, moreover, was benefiting more and more from misplaced ammunition drops which they retrieved while the few remaining French guns were becoming starved of shells.

To the south of the main complex another isolated garrison, "Isabelle," held out alone, but was being steadily enmeshed by the saps and trenches of the enemy, much as their comrades to the north had been. Almost completely cut off from their fellow defenders around the now useless airstrip, the garrison of Isabelle fought on in their own private war, although they still had the bulk of the heavy guns which were used to support the main fortress. As the enemy mined closer, the trenches were turned into underground galleries and forts of their own, from which sudden massed assaults could be thrown in time after time with hardly any warning. The navy Helldivers were continually being called upon to try and smash these strong fortifications on the very edge of the friendly forces' wire. Only precision attacks of the highest order could have done the job at all. The overall area of Isabelle was, of course, far smaller than even Dien Bien Phu itself, so massed aerial high-altitude bombing was out of the question, even had the means to provide it existed.

Attack followed attack and losses grew. On 4 April a heavy enemy assault was repulsed with the loss of 2,000 Communist dead and this part of the battle alone was estimated to have cost Giap some 10,000 casualties in all. On 9 April two SB-2Cs made a low-level sortie along Road 41B seeking out and destroying Vietminh supply convoys approaching the battle. They were taken under heavy and accurate fire by 37-mm batteries concentrated around strongpoint Beatrice. The leading Helldiver, piloted by Lieutenant de la Ferrier, managed to bore right through the tracer and shells unscathed at zero feet and escape from this trap. His wingman, Ensign Jean Marie Laugier, was not so fortunate. Hit repeatedly, the second dive-bomber went into the ground followed all the way down by more shell bursts. Even had there been survivors, the wreck was deep within enemy-occupied jungle and they could not have been rescued by the grieving paratroops.

It should not be thought that all the dive-bombers' efforts at cutting the enemy supply routes were total failures. One Vietminh deserter, from their 209 Regiment, clearly stated that supplies had been harder and harder to obtain due to such "road cuts." Losses among the hapless and defenseless *da cong* human mules must have been very heavy indeed. Nonetheless, by now the Vietminh had three hundred guns in position when the French believed they had only sixty.

Another counterattack was launched by the French garrison at dawn on 10 April, against strongpoint "Elaine-1." The leading assault troops went "over the top" in true World War I style at 0610 that morning and were aided by the navy dive-bombers which attacked precisely on schedule. Four Helldivers dropped twelve 500-pound bombs and two 1,000-pound bombs in the first attack a bare four hundred meters from Elaine-1, close support at its best. A second quartet put sixteen 500-pound bombs down around Beatrice. Their bombs and napalm loads smashed down on the enemy support units lurking in the gullies and trenches to the west of the battlefield, thus sealing the enemy defenders off from reinforcements at a critical juncture.

The enemy responded in kind with a heavy artillery barrage, and for a while it was touch and go. Finally additional French troops, equipped with flame throwers, tipped the scales and the Vietminh were wiped out on Elaine-1. The Helldivers returned to help mop up by decimating what was left of an enemy battalion still resisting on nearby "Phoney Mountain," a dominant hill overlooking the front. The excellent close air support work in this day's operations earned the Helldiver squadron a special citation from General de Castries himself. This was to prove the high point of the French defense.

The remorseless enemy sapping had continued and now it was the turn of the northern strongpoints to disappear in their cold embrace. "Huguette-1," the most northerly, was cut off from the rest of the command with only shell-swept wastes of an airfield, itself already bisected by further enemy trenches and concealed machine-gun nests. A desperate attempt to break out was planned for dawn on Easter Monday, 19 April 1954. In preparations the day before, the Helldivers once again earned the accolades of the ground troops for their accuracy. They planted their ordnance exactly in the tiny 200-meter gap that separated the cutoff post and friendly positions. At heavy cost the little garrison broke through, but the ring was pulled even tighter around the survivors.

As the trap finally closed and the fate of the garrison became inevitable, the anger and frustration of the defenders turned more and more to the staff officers back in the safety of Hanoi. These, it was felt, had no conception of what the defenders were enduring or how to help them. Bitter comments were also made about the air support being received, although the charges were those of "excessive prudence." However, their regard for the navy dive-bomber air crews was in no way diminished and they explicitly exempted the Helldivers from any such allegations.

The end was now rapidly approaching. The defenders were exhausted both mentally and physically. There was no place to hide from the continuous shelling, the troops melted away in attack after attack, and replacements of men, material, and ammunition continued to fall. The loss of Huguette-1 had reduced the already-minute area of the supply-dropping zone by half, and it was decided to take a desperate gamble to relieve this situation by making another counterattack. By this time finding sufficient fit troops for such an attack proved very difficult. The openness of the terrain itself was to prove deadly for such an effort.

Still the attempt was made, at 1400 on 23 April. The Vietminh regiment defending the position was dive-bombed by 11F and almost entirely wiped out. Four Helldivers carried out the first sortie but their eight 1,000-pound bombs were not so accurately delivered on this occasion due to the hail of flak that met them. Two more Helldivers followed them in and this time their heavy bombs were delivered precisely into the enemy trenches east of Huguette-6, the exactness of their placing drawing appreciative radio signals from the French troops close by. A further vertical attack was then made in classic style by two more SB-2Cs, which hit Vietminh troops occupying Huguette-7. Their attack dives were made at almost 90 degrees down from 8,000 feet and 6,000 feet to point-blank range, and the four heavy bombs landed exactly on target, duly obliterating the enemy infantry.

This attack on Huguette-1 had been devastating indeed. But when the paratroops emerged to cross the open ground between the positions and the smoking and defenderless strongpoint, they immediately ran into heavy cross fire from an unsuspected machine-gun nest hidden in a wrecked aircraft on the runway's edge. The attack faltered and stopped. The Communist artillery joined in and the flak gunners turned their weapons away from the aircraft and swept the runway. There was nothing left but withdrawal, and the day ended in failure for the French.

The Helldivers continued to give support during the final days of the battle but were not in on the final debacle because the involvement of the Helldivers ended on 30 April when the *Arromanches* was relieved off Indochina by the carrier *Bois Bellieu* (under Captain Mornu). The Helldivers were exchanged between the two ships for the Chance Vought Corsairs of 11F. Unit 3 F had conducted 186 sorties or flown 283 hours of combat time during this last period. From 24 May when they had reembarked aboard the carrier until 2 June they had dropped 372,700 pounds of bombs and fired 4,350 rounds of 20-mm cannon shell while strafing. Four of the nine SB-2Cs embarked by the *Bois Bellieu*, having remained operational for a time until 2 June, did patrol work before that vessel left for Hong Kong. The detachment of Helldivers working out of Bach Mai continued flying. On 1 May they flew nine sorties in conjunction with Operation "Castor" at Dien Bien Phu and other missions against Hill 13 at Thai Nguyen. Further missions took place in May, led by Lieutenant Bellone, objectives including positions at Yen Bay and Cat Bi, while all nine were fit by 6 May to strike at Hill 41 by Tuan Giao. On 7 May the *Bois Bellieu* launched a heavy strike of twelve SB-2Cs to hit

Vietminh troops during the final winding up of the ill-fated Operation Castor. These were the last carrier-based strikes, but the Bach Mai contingent continued work on their own. On 9 May four sorties were flown against Son La, on 10 May two against Thai Nguyen and four more against villages near Haidong. Next another four were flown against Ye Bay, and on 12 May the Helldivers were once again active with four strikes against Hill 41 and four against a Vietminh battalion caught in the open two kilometers southwest of Phuly; a further four sorties were flown against the village of Binh Tru, twenty kilometers east of Hanoi, which showed how close and how bold the enemy had become since their victory, and how they intended to gain as much land as possible prior to the armistice. Three more sorties were mounted against the village of Nhiep Xa and a final three against a village south of Phuly once more, giving a total of eighteen sorties in one day, three per operational Helldiver.

This continued to be the pattern from 13 May through to 25 May. It was the end of a long period of honorable service for the Curtiss SB-2C. Those aircraft that did not return to France aboard the carriers remained in service as training machines, their places in the front line taken over by Chance Vought F-4U Corsairs until the war came to its end with the division of Vietnam on 21 July 1954. However, this proved to be the end of the war only as far as the French were concerned. For Giap and Ho-Chi-Minh it was merely a breather to reorganize the infiltration and conquest of the democratic southern part of that unhappy nation in order to bring it totally under the Communist yoke.

Meanwhile a similar Communist expansion had erupted over another arbitrary border, that between North and South Korea, when the former launched a full-scale invasion of the latter on 25 June 1950. For the first and only time in its entire history the United Nations stood firm against Communist aggression.

The war was by no means a war of movement. The initial Communist thrust was halted and reversed. The Chinese intervention in turn tipped the balance back again. In the bleak, cold mountain wastes of central Korea the opposing battle lines developed into something closely resembling the ghastly trench warfare of 1915–18. All the old lessons of close support had to be relearned yet again by a new generation of fliers.

The weapons used by the ground-attack aircraft were those still in place from World War II. The most effective was napalm, which had been used during 1945 and had initially been known as "blaze bombs." Simple to construct, they were merely auxiliary fuel pods whose contents consisted of a substance like dry gelatin mixed with gasoline, which

When the Korean War erupted with the invasion of South Korea by the Communist Northern armies, the quickest response the United Nations forces could make was to send in the aircraft carriers of American and British fleets. Here a Hawker Sea Fury prepares to take off for a strike mission from a British carrier. Note the resurrection of the old Allied "Invasion Stripe" markings and the rocket tubes fitted below the wings, with additional clusters on the folded outboard wing sections of those lined up on the deck behind. (Author's collection, courtesy of Tom Harrington)

The Korean War proved that the lessons of World War II were still valid in the jet age. Although the new breed of fighter aircraft could not linger in the target zone like their propeller-driven cousins, the employment of such aircraft as the Thunderchief proved vital in bridge-smashing operations and other tactical deployments with bombs or napalm. (Smithsonian Institution, Washington, DC)

formed a highly inflammable petroleum jelly. The pod was fitted with a fused igniter. Initial shortages of both the jelly's ingredients and the wing tanks to carry them into battle prevented napalm's widespread use in Korea at first, but when these were resolved it soon became the favored weapon of ground support.

On impact the blazing jelly quickly spread and, burning at temperatures of 2,000 degrees centigrade, covered an area as large as 100 by 200 feet. It had the tendency to cling in lumps to the target, which increased its effect (and horror). Against massed tanks its main advantages were that it destroyed the insulation in the electrical wiring, burned the rubber off the bogie wheels, exploded the ammunition, and cremated the crew by penetrating any open space. Its limitation at the front was that it had to be used within twenty-four hours of mixing or the mass separated and became useless.

Regarding its all too obvious practical effects it is recorded that on the drive north to Seoul the UN forces found ample evidence in columns and lines of "burned-out tanks, trucks and gun emplacements. Enemy soldiers still crouched in the attitudes in which the firey death found them."[7]

The 5-inch rocket, an upgrade from the 3-inch version, also originally introduced toward the end of 1944, was still valued against vehicles rather than personnel. Essentially an antitank weapon, it was thought to be useless against the Soviet-built T.34s, but combat experience in Korea showed that, properly used, it *could* penetrate their armor. But to compensate for early failures, a 6½-inch rocket was hastily designed. It had a shaped charge which concentrated the explosive force forward to blow a hole through tank armor plate. Both rockets had the same motor, which proved inadequate, and of course the old problem of inaccuracy persisted.

General-purpose and fragmentation bombs continued to be the main antiinfantry weapon, with improved proximity fuses on fragmentation bombs. None of the very specialized antiinfantry weapons developed by the Germans and the Soviets on the Eastern Front was reintroduced by the UN forces. Finally, cannon and machine-gun strafing raids continued to be employed, as they had been from the very beginnings of aerial warfare.

US Army Major Michael J. Dolan was to analyze the situation at the start of the war and its developments in the first year of conflict thus: "Air power alone hasn't won a single action against ground troops. But the infantry will be the first to rise up and say that the combination of tactical air and on-the-ground fighting has won many a fight. They will also say that when the weather prevented air support, the infantry found its attack stalled, or had to give ground to an enemy that a few well-placed napalm bombs could have defeated."[8]

In the aftermath of World War II the belief in the close air support concept had waned. The splitting of the air force from the army had taken place in the United States in 1947, and this led to the same polarization as it had in Great Britain in 1918. Only the US Marine Corps continued to appreciate the great value of close tactical aviation. The marine fliers continued to enhance the dedicated expertise they had established in the Philippines, and they further developed their skilled air-to-ground techniques almost single-handedly, achieving a very high standard of proficiency.

Apart from that, only a kernel of close-support theory was kept faintly alive by the setting up of a Joint Operations Center (JOC) at Pope Field, Fort Bragg, North Carolina. This was staffed both by army personnel from V Corps and air force pilots from Langley Air Force Base, Virginia. This small team kept the flame of close tactical air support flickering. In Dolan's words they

> tested, revised and re-tested in field exercises, such as "Portrex" and "Swarmer." Meanwhile, at service schools of both the Army and the Air Force some thought was given to tactical air doctrine in lectures and occasional demonstrations. But each school had its own ideas. . . .
>
> Exercises "Swarmer" and "Portrex" pointed up the need for the training of the Army in the use of air power in support of ground attacks. A program for such training was then developed. This came belatedly. The implementing document was hardly printed when we found ourselves involved in Korea. . . .[9]

When General Mark W. Clark was questioned on exactly what kind of air support the army required, his answers sounded almost identical to those of General Sir Edmund Ironside in 1940, and of many other military commanders all through World War II.

"The aircraft which is to provide close tactical support should be designed specifically for that mission and not be compromised by a primary requirement to engage in air-to-air battles." He went on to state, "Ideally, tactical support designs should be the coordinated effort of both ground officers (who can state the 'requirement' just as they would state the requirement for an artillery piece) and air officers (who can reconcile these requirements with engineering limitations)."[10]

He also gave a general specification on an "ideal" ground-support aircraft for Korean conditions. "Such a machine should be able to carry

The ubiquitous Douglas Skyraider, a.k.a. the "Spad," the "Heavy Hauler," or the "Able Dog," operated from carrier decks and jungle airstrips alike for almost thirty years, mounting strike upon strike against Communist aggression in Korea and Vietnam. Long after piston-engine aircraft had been declared obsolete, the Skyraider's enormous ordnance-lifting power, its ability to strike at small targets accurately, and, above all, its ability to "loiter" in the target zone awaiting targets of opportunity at the request of ground troops, were everything required in a close-support airplane. (Official US Navy photo, Washington, DC)

a 9,000-pound load of ammunition, bombs, rockets, and bullets; have sufficient accuracy and stability to hit the target; have adequate communications with ground officers directing their strikes; carry enough fuel to give it at least two hours over the battle area; take off in 3,000 feet; and operate in any kind of weather, day or night."[11]

In other words, what the soldiers still required was what the German Stuka, RAF Vengeance, and Soviet Pe-2 had always given—accuracy, ability to linger over the target, and almost immediate availability. What the air force actually provided to do the same job were machines whose first requirement was to "live in the air." Reminiscent of the RAF's obsession with fast fighter-bombers in World War II, speed and the ability to double as a fighter were the airmen's priority.

In Korea the battle of speed over accuracy was just as bitter as in North Africa in 1942–43, but more so because now the US Air Force was utilizing jet aircraft. These were mainly Lockheed F-80 Shooting Stars and Republic F-84 Thunderjets, straight-wing jet fighters that had proved themselves outclassed by the MiG-15 and had been replaced in the pure fighter role by the North American F-86 Sabre. Initially also, propeller-driven aircraft had been utilized in the ground-attack role. The supreme Chance Vought F-4U Corsair and the North American P-51 Mustang made brief comebacks in this role and won a new lease on life, together with newer types like the American Douglas Skyraider and the British navy's Hawker Sea Fury, both the latter flying from carriers off the coast of Korea, and the French air force's Grumman Bearcats in Indochina.

137

Eastern Bloc nations modernized their ground-attack units as part of the Warsaw Pact, using Soviet-supplied aircraft and weapons to achieve harmony of purpose. Here a Polish ground crew arms a MiG-21 fighter-bomber for a close-support mission during exercises in the 1960s. (Author's collection)

General Mark W. Clark himself flew combat missions in both propeller and jet attack aircraft to get a true perspective. He reported:

> So far as striking the target, I was convinced that the jet could do just as good a job as the piston-type plane. The trouble was that too many jet pilots refused to slow their planes down long enough over the target area to get the required accuracy. It wasn't that they couldn't slow down, it was just that they preferred to get in quick and get out of there.
>
> To the guy on the ground it doesn't make much sense for a fighter-bomber to come within a few miles of its target only to jettison its bomb load and go upstairs to fend off an attacking fighter force. Once committed to a task, say the ground men, the fighters should stick with it to the end.[12]

It was not merely a matter of the whole mission being a waste of time and effort if the bomb load was not accurately placed. Precision was required not just to hit the enemy where it mattered but also to avoid hitting one's own forces. Army confidence in close support had been severely weakened in World War II by fighter-bombers in low-level runs overshooting and hitting their own men. In Korea this was to happen again. On 10 September 1950 the British Argyll and Sutherland Highlanders were dug in under the shadow of Chinese regiments on a hill overlooking Naktong. They called in an air strike to take the pressure off and laid out indicator panels in front of their lines to help the airmen identify their own positions.

The Chinese had seen this done before and merely duplicated the markings. In a properly directed and controlled strike this would have made matters difficult but not impossible. However, the state of the art had either been forgotten, or not returned to its World War II peak. Dive-bombing was not attempted; instead low-level runs were made by American P-51 Mustangs, which hit the wrong hill. As a result the Argylls took heavy losses from their own allies, and sixty men were killed or wounded. As well as the human tragedy of such an incident, word spread and British troops were hardly likely to call on the airmen again, no matter how hard pressed they were.

The air force stated that during the first seventy-five days of operations in Korea, close air support of ground forces had consumed two-thirds of the total sortie capability of the Far East Air Forces. "This preoccupation with the close support mission stemmed chiefly from our having to piecemeal our ground forces into battle under very unfavorable circumstances," they claimed.[13] Nor was it admitted that jets were less efficient at close air support than prop planes. General Hoyt S. Vandenberg stated unreservedly that: "Jets are superior for every conceivable job demanded of a fighter plane, including flying at tree-top level to silence one machine gun."[14]

The American air force could also point to the fact that the new F-84E jet was capable of carrying thirty-two 6½-inch rockets whereas the old propeller-driven F-51 could lift only eight into combat.

But this was missing the point that for close support "every conceivable job demanded of a *fighter*" was irrelevant. The American air force also claimed that fitting enlarged wing-tip fuel tanks to the jets "gave the F-80 all usable flight duration. It was capable of all the deceleration it needed. It carried large armament loads and it provided a weapons platform of great stability."[15]

The contrast between the dedicated methods of the Marine Corps fliers and those of the army was given voice by ground troops. *Air Force* magazine quoted three anonymous press reports: July 1950: "What was needed, of course, was a couple of old-fashioned Marine Divisions with their integrated Air Force."[16]

19 August 1950: "We want no more of these jet jockeys. They don't have enough fuel to stay in our areas long enough to find out where we are having trouble. And they don't have enough fire power to do any real good. Give us those Marines."[17]

26 November 1950: "A lot of GIs in Korea are wishing for a big 'umbrella' like the one 'issued' the Marines when they go out in a storm."[18]

Finally, on 3 November 1950: "None of the Air Force or Army officers here know how to go about setting up a system for close support of ground troops . . . there were no trained officers who knew how to direct airplanes that were supposed to provide close support."[19]

Both sides of the argument agreed that air power, being the most flexible of the many weapons available, was the most suitable one to employ. In range, speed, and firepower it had no equal. But all these assets were of no value if they could not be directed to where they were needed. The air force system was the "Big Battalions" approach. In the main combat zone the ground and air commanders each controlled his own force but planning was done jointly. Thus, corresponding to an army group and an individual army were the Tactical Air Command and numbered air force. With this system the air force commander could move his entire force to the vital spot, similar to the old Luftwaffe method of concentrating everything at point of contact.

Opposed to this method was the call for a system that would provide each army force, right down to divisional level, with its own fixed number of airplanes to use as it saw fit to suit local conditions. Time of response and accuracy would, it was claimed, be superior and less cumbersome. Exponents of this method pointed to the success of the Marine Corps in Korea compared to the rest of the air/ground forces.

The air force countered by saying that they were responsible for interdiction and air superiority targets as well as close support, whereas the marine air arm concentrated almost exclusively on one assignment—close support. Exactly, and that's why they are superior, came the reply. The air force gave out figures that proved that 76 percent of sorties were flown by them as against 14 percent by the navy and 10 percent by the marines. Their opponents countered by saying that if the navy and Marine Corps' 24 percent mainly hit the targets whereas the air force's 76 percent missed it, then it was not the totals that counted, but how they were applied. And so it continued.

Away from theory and back on the ground in actual combat, progress was made. On 3 July 1950, the first JOC was established. Initially it was little more than an expanded Tactical Air Control Party (TACP), but the first forward air controller joined the advance elements of 24 Infantry Division and this was a watershed in ground support. At Divisional Command an air liaison officer (ALO) worked hand in glove with G-3 Air. Fully operational by 19 July, the JOC's biggest handicap was getting suitable and sufficient radio sets. Suitable because the mountainous terrain of the battlefield, combined with inexperienced operators, prevented the proper use of voice radio. Initially, therefore, air-support requests had to be made via encoded signals sent by wire, with resulting delay of hours. This of course rendered the whole system point-

A common "behind-the-front" scene that could be anywhere in the world as a fighter-bomber is loaded with heavy bombs and refueled under its protective camouflage netting. In this case it is a practice for a SAAB 32A jet at a field base in northeast Sweden in 1967. (Nils Kindberg, Stockholm)

less, for the conditions on the ground had changed by the time the aircraft arrived.

The only other equipment available was the four-channel SCR 522 radio, a World War II leftover with few spares. Other equipment included a VHF transceiver and the High Frequency SCR 191 radio. Both these sets were carried on the backseat of a small truck, but they proved fragile in combat conditions, even when cushioned with army blankets. The only reliable alternative was a SCR 399 radio carried in a truck. Dynamotors burned out after a period of twelve-hour-a-day usage. What was desperately needed was a lightweight outfit, rugged and reliable.

Small "spotter" planes, L-5 liaison aircraft, with VHF radios were able to act as airborne controllers and directors of strikes. Later they were joined, and then replaced, by North American armed T-6 "Mosquito" aircraft, with an air force pilot and a trained army observer aboard. These aircraft patrolled defined sectors so that they became totally familiar with the terrain they were covering. They combined with the TACPs in jeeps to give front-line coverage, while the JOCs coordinated their reports. The arrival of highly trained radio operators from 20 Signal Air-Ground Liaison Company in October 1950, along with better equipment and telephone "patches," made direct voice contact between JOC and Division possible.

Each TACP consisted of an experienced air force pilot and two airmen, one the radio operator and the other a radio technician to keep the set in working condition. The original Spartan allotment of one TACP to an army division was increased to one to each regiment plus a Division Net Control team. Tours of duty were finally extended to three weeks per team, again so they could get to know in detail both the terrain and the army units they were covering.

All these changes vastly improved matters and the army chief of staff, General J. Lawton Collins, was able to state with relief, "Now the system works."[20]

But it was with armored units that the system fell down. Although each division's heavy tank battalion had an ANARC 3 VHF radio, there was, incredibly, no corresponding allocation of VHF radio operators or engineers. It was left for individual divisions to jury-rig their own arrangements. One tank battalion equipped a special tank with two common frequency channels so they could monitor aircraft talk. Thus tank columns were totally reliant on their infantry support. In Korea, where the role of the tank was limited, this was not so important, but what that situation forebode for mobile warfare in Europe was ominous.

With the front stabilizing into a static trench system across the peninsula, a "bomb line" was established, exactly as had been done in Italy in the 1943–44 period. This line had to be based on visually recognizable features that were readily identifiable from the air: rivers, tracks, and mountain ridges. In Korea the bomb line ("Green Line") was marked out to run at least 1,000 yards beyond the most advanced troop positions on the ground. Beyond this zone air strikes could be made at will, but within it, air attacks would be conducted only when sanctioned by either air or ground controllers.

Unfortunately, friendly target marking was far from foolproof, as we have seen. Utilizing two-foot-square red cloth marker panels in coded groups was tried, but the enemy soon duplicated the patterns.

Conversely, indication of potential targets also posed problems. In Burma in 1944 the RAF Vengeances had been guided to their objectives by patterns of smoke fired from mortars. But the smoke tended to drift, and the enemy also laid smoke, even duplicating different colors. In

Korea there was no jungle, but the Communists were just as brilliant at hiding their guns, tanks, and infantry as the Japanese had been in Burma and the Vietminh were proving to be in Indochina.

Smoke bombs dropped by the circling T-6s were used by the Americans as were wing-mounted smoke rockets fired into the target. Artillery-fired phosphorus shells were the most widely used target-marking method in Korea, but suffered the same drawbacks of the smoke drifting or being duplicated by the enemy.

Despite its severe limitations, close air support was proven essential, even in the comparatively static battle zone that Korea became up to the final cease-fire. Old lessons had been painfully reabsorbed, old mistakes made and rectified, old arguments rekindled and refought. But at the end of it all, direct ground support of troops was recognized as being essential and indeed the major part of a working wartime air force.

The atomic bomb and political limitations on the use of strategical air power beyond carefully defined limits had placed two frustrating, but avoidable, blocks on unrestricted air power. With the coming of these constraints all the old visions of Trenchard, Mitchell, Douhet, and Harris finally died. From the 1950s the air forces knew that, far from considering supporting the army from the air as being "beneath their dignity," as they did in the 1930s, if they were to have any meaningful role at all in "limited" or "brush-fire" wars, they had to be in the close-support business 100 percent!

The superb lines of the F-86D. This machine, FU-863 "Dennis the Menace," shows off the mid-1960s jet fighter-bomber as developed by the USAF after their experience in Korea. (Gerald Balzer)

eight

New Lessons and Microchip Technology

There have been many wars since Korea in which tanks, infantry, and fixed-wing aircraft have acted in mutual support of one another in battle. Indeed it is almost unthinkable for aircraft not to be involved in modern battles, although as we move into the 1990s that ability is again severely questioned. We can only briefly examine a few such battles as fairly typical examples of them all.

The most traumatic in casualties, influence, and results was of course Vietnam. The Viet Cong (VC) insurgents were raised by Hanoi as part of their ploy to take over the whole country, and South Vietnam proved unable to cope. Two-thirds of the country was in Communist hands by the end of 1964.

The United States became officially involved in Vietnam on 2 August 1964 when its warships on patrol in international waters were attacked by North Vietnamese torpedo boats. Several squadrons of F-100 and F-102 fighter-bombers were flown into Da Nang air base and Takhli. From then on they were sucked steadily deeper into the war. In effect it resembled the Spanish Civil War in that both East and West used it as a proving ground for their latest weapons technology. In another way it resembled Korea because in the south at least the Americans had overwhelming air superiority which they could use to blanket the enemy if they could catch him in the open. It also of course resembled the French experience in the same region in that the Communists proved elu-

sive, and that a normal air-interdiction campaign against a native supply line was of limited effectiveness.

Before American withdrawal, close air support to the land troops had been provided on a lavish and unprecedented scale. From old propeller-driven Douglas A-1 Skyraiders of the Vietnamese air force (VNAF) to the latest air force and navy jets like the F-105D Thunderchief (or "Thud"), Douglas A-4 Skyhawk, Vought A-7 Corsair, and McDonnell F-4D Phantom and an impressive array of helicopter gunships (which fall outside the scope of this book), the US, South Vietnamese, Australian, and Philippine ground troops could call on an enormous array of air power to assist them.

One good example of early close-support work in Vietnam took place in June 1965 at Dong Xoai, in Phuoc Long Province, some fifty miles north from the capital, Saigon. This was a "Special Forces" camp. In the early hours of 10 June an entire VC regiment attacked the four-hundred-strong defense, which included twenty-eight US special forces men and nine marine Seabee construction personnel. Half the compound was overrun, and the defenses were surrounded, outgunned, and outnumbered. Low clouds prevented the VNAF A-1Hs called to the scene from intervening despite flare-dropping from a C-47 transport.

At 0430 two USAF-piloted A-1Es were scrambled from Bien Hoa airbase. Although cloud cover was down to 500 feet the two pilots, Captain Richard Y. Costain and Captain Doyle C. Ruff, unhesitatingly went

As in Korea and elsewhere, although jet aircraft were used predominantly for air strikes to good effect, there was still a need for an aircraft that could carry large amounts of heavy ordnance and still have the ability to linger in the target zone. The whole rationale of the Stuka and the Dauntless in World War II was still a valid concept two decades later. The last of the dive-bombers in this classic tradition was the Douglas Skyraider (seen here fully loaded over South Vietnam in 1965) and later adaptations of the old "Able Dog" served well. (Official US Air Force photo, Washington, DC)

The harsh lessons of fighting against a largely unseen and clandestine opponent in heavy jungle had been learned in Burma and the Pacific against the Japanese. The lessons of fighting against a tenacious and politically indoctrinated enemy were absorbed in Korea. The Communists continued to use these tactics in their conquest of South Vietnam. Only the US, South Korea, the Philippines, and Australia stood up to this latest takeover, and so close air support was principally supplied by the American navy, marines, and air force while the South Vietnamese air force was trained. Continuous air support was found to be essential to hold outposts and prevent another Dien Bien Phu. Thanks to intensive flying by the young American pilots and an enormous application of manpower and hardware, the line was held.

Half the problem in jungle fighting is locating the enemy so he can be hit. Here a forward-air-controller flying in a USAF O-1E "Bird Dog" aircraft is on the way to the target area during Operation "Pink Rose," which took place in Vietnam in 1967. (Official Air Force photo, Washington, DC)

Here a USAF DV-10 "Bronco" reconnaissance plane illustrates the best features of spotter aircraft—good all-round vision and slow speed to enable it to hover and study the terrain. These features, of course, also made them vulnerable to light antiaircraft fire from the ground, even in those days before hand-held missiles had proliferated. (Official US Air Force photo, Washington, DC)

into the attack using instrument flying. Each A-1E carried twelve 260-pound fragmentation bombs under their wings. The minimum safe altitude for dropping these was 1,000 feet. They both made direct hits and during the rest of the day continuous air strikes were conducted which finally broke the enemy and lifted the siege.

By mid-1966 there were 250 forward air controllers (FACs) working over South Vietnam's forty-three provinces, equipped with 150 Cessna O-1s. Each of these "Bird Dogs" was equipped with four smoke or white phosphorus rockets for target marking. Each flight was three to four hours long. The bulk of this time was spent at between 1,000 to 1,500 feet on visual reconnaissance (VR) hunting the Viet Cong. If the enemy was spotted, a special procedure had to be gone through before any air strike could be called up.

The FAC had to report his findings to both the Direct Air Support Center (DASC) at corps Headquarters and the local Vietnamese province chief. The latter had to give his personal authorization for any strike to be made at suspected guerrilla groups, in order to prevent hitting innocent civilians. Only then could the FAC guide in the strike aircraft to the target. The Cessnas were highly vulnerable to ground fire however, being brought down by even rifle or automatic machine-gun fire. Twelve Bird Dogs were shot down in 1965, four times that number the next year.

To replace them the US Air Force brought in the much more powerful North American OV-10A aircraft. This was a twin-boom, twin-engine, high-wing two-seater. Known as the COIN (Counter-Insurgency) aircraft, they entered service in 1967. The design incorporated lightweight armor for crew protection, increased the smoke rockets to eight, and included provisions for eight flares for night operations and a 7.62-mm Minigun pod to strafe "targets of opportunity." It was like watching the 1914–15 developments starting anew.

Along with greater lifting power, armament, and protection, the COIN aircraft naturally carried increasingly sophisticated communications equipment. Each machine carried an IFF (Identification Friend or Foe) transmitter to allow ground radar to plot its positions and two FM, one VHF, and one UHF radio to allow better links with the army sets, such as the PRC-25 "backpack" sets carried by infantry.

The enemy was a past master at the use of light, mobile antiaircraft guns in his own protection, of course. These highly sophisticated, splendidly coordinated, radar-controlled batteries were far from the TV image of natives armed with bicycles and rifles. They ranged from the deadly close-range quadruple mobile 14.5-mm heavy machine gun, optically guided up to 2,000 feet, through to 37-mm, 57-mm, 88-mm, and 100-mm cannon which could range from 4,500 feet to 20,000 feet. The North Vietnamese had more than two thousand guns at the start. By 1966 they had built up to five thousand guns and then increased to seven thousand guns the next year.

These antiaircraft weapons made conventional close support a hazardous business. Bombing was directed to take place from between 4,000 and 5,000 feet, which ruined accuracy. Only one pass over the target was advisable since the flak soon locked on to a series of bomb strikes. The North Vietnamese also had sufficient resources behind them to permit the firing of blind barrages by massed antiaircraft batteries on a preset bearing and height, through which the ground-support aircraft had to fly. The harsh verdict was that to fly under 3,500 feet was suicidal.

Once the enemy had been located, detailed and painstaking planning had to be done to ensure the air strikes hit the correct targets. Close coordination between the troops on the ground and the fliers was always vital. The scene is An Khe, South Vietnam, and US Air Force and Army officers work together on forward air control support for the US Army's 1 Cavalry Division's next mission in July 1966. (Official US Air Force photo, Washington, DC)

It was a very effective counter, and antiaircraft fire was responsible for 85 percent of all American aircraft losses in the war. It soon became a technology war too, with American EB-66C "Brown Cradle" aircraft being used to transmit jamming signals to block out the enemy radar pulses. An emergency program was begun to install passive and active electronic counter equipment in all close-support aircraft. This program was hastened by the fact that the Soviets also began shipping SA-2 "Guideline" surface-to-air missiles (SAM) to the Viet Cong that had a slant range over twenty-three miles and an effective hitting height of 60,000 feet.

The American ground-attack aircraft developed the "pop-up" technique of approaching the target at only a few hundred feet above ground level, popping up to a higher altitude just before striking to enable their radar to lock onto the target, and releasing their bombs.

Most of these tactics were necessary when attacking targets north of the so-called Demilitarized Zone (DMZ); for ground attacks in the south, the light flak remained the main threat. While conventional bombs, napalm, and rockets continued to be employed, the Americans began introducing "standoff" weapons to defeat the enemy antiaircraft systems. In March 1967 came the first use of the air-to-ground (AGM) weapon AGM-62, or "Walleye." This was a glide bomb directed right to the target by a television guidance system, but again these were more suitable for interdiction attacks than for direct ground support in the field.

In Vietnam the North Vietnamese troops were hidden by the lush tropical jungle and rarely committed themselves to set-piece battles. All manner of sensors were employed to detect the enemy and defeat them, but like the French before them, the Americans needed a substantial target at which to strike to fully utilize their close-support air power. Such an opportunity came in January 1968 when, trying for another Dien Bien Phu victory, General Giap threw North Vietnamese divisions against an isolated US Marine base at Khe Sanh. This time he was not up against a handful of Helldivers but the whole might of the US Tactical Air Force.

Operation "Scotland" called for the US 26th Marines to conduct a regimental-size operation to defend the Khe Sanh airfield and base area with minimum forces and maximum use of obstacles and supporting fire. It was, in effect, a Dien Bien Phu "come-on," designed to draw in the North Vietnamese regulars so they could be slaughtered. They duly complied.

In their own defense the Marine Air Wing flew 967 sorties with fixed-wing aircraft, delivering 1,961 tons of bombs. As the official report stated: "The amount of air and artillery support that the 26th

Marines received during the defense of Khe Sanh was enormous. Few regiments ever had such an overwhelming amount of firepower at their disposal."[1]

Requests for air support came from the Field Support Control Center (FSCC) which had both artillery and artillery representatives as an integral part of the regimental staff. The FSCC planned and supervised the execution of all fire missions within the Scotland area of operations. Subordinate to the FSCC was the Khe Sanh Direct Air Support Center (DASC) under Major Charles D. Goddard. Requests for air support from the FSCC were channeled through the DASC to the Tactical Air Direction Center (TADC) of the 1st Marine Air Wing (MAW). Whenever the wing could not completely fill a quota, liaison teams within the DASC called on the other services for assistance. Once the schedule was met and the strike aircraft had arrived on station, the Marine DASC, aided by Airborne Command and Control Center (ABCC) from 7th Air Force, coordinated all the air operations within the Khe Sanh Tactical Area of Operations (TAOR).

This gigantic air umbrella, so typical of the Marines' dedicated approach, was codenamed Operation "Niagara" and lasted from 22 January until 31 March. Air elements involved included the 1st MAW, 7th Air Force, Vietnamese air force, and others, but by far and away the majority of the sorties were flown by US marine, navy, and air force crews. Their mission was "to destroy enemy force in the Scotland TAOR, interdict enemy supply lines and base area, and provide maximum tactical air support to friendly forces."[2]

Close air support missions were utilized against pinpoint targets in the proximity of friendly troops. It was found that this type of air strike was the most responsive to the needs of the ground commanders and the most accurate. Nearly always there were fighter-bombers patrolling over Khe Sanh around the clock. Other aircraft were at instant readiness on "hot pads" where they could be quickly scrambled, and yet more could be diverted from other missions at short notice. The Marine Air Wing procedures during this battle were indicative of close air support at its best and are worthy of closer study.

Upon arrival on station, each pilot checked in with the DASC and was then handed over to one of seven marine or air force tactical air controllers (airborne), TAC(A)s, who personally directed the strike. The air force personnel were members of 20 Tactical Air Support Squadron and the marines came from Headquarters and Maintenance Squadron 14 and Marine Observation Squadron 6. At least five of the pilots remained airborne over the battlefield in their Cessna O1-E "Bird Dog" observation aircraft or UH-1E helicopter gunships during the hours of daylight. They maintained direct communication with both the attack aircraft and the troops on the ground. Thus these TAC(A)s could rapidly deploy the jets wherever they were required and their close supervision reduced the chances of accidentally hitting their own men.

When a flight arrived on station, the DASC normally directed it to a holding pattern until a TAC(A) or a forward air controller on the ground was free to handle the strike. "These patterns sometimes extended up to 35,000 feet with scores of planes gradually augering their way downward as each preceding flight unloaded its ordnance and scooted for home."[3]

Once a TAC(A) had picked out a worthwhile target, or was assigned one by the FSCC, he cleared the strike aircraft into his own area. The pilots then broke formation and dropped down to attack level through the haze, dust, and cloud layers that covered the battlefield. One hazard was keeping clear of the low-flying camouflaged Bird Dogs and Hueys themselves. Most attack aircraft used their automatic direction finders to get a fix on the TAC(A)s' radio transmissions. As they sorted themselves out, a continual ongoing update of the target location and description was being passed to them, including details of expected flak resistance, nearest friendly forces, and wind speed over the target.

Visual contact between the controller and his flight established, the TAC(A) would order aircraft to make a marking run over the target which the aircraft would pinpoint by firing a smoke rocket or lobbing a colored-smoke grenade. The attack pilots would note this but would also mark the TAC(A)'s position and that of their own nearest ground troops before commencing the run. Again, prior to the actual assault and provided that enemy antiaircraft positions had been surpressed satisfactorily, a few dummy passes would be made over the target, until the controller was satisfied they had the correct target lined up. When he was satisfied he cleared the attack pilots for a "hot" pass.

As they attacked, the TAC(A) would monitor his VHF tactical net to the ground troops and give short corrections to the attack pilots over his UHF radio. Attack runs would be continued until the aircraft were "high and dry" or "ammo minus" (both of which meant all ordnance had been expended). In the wake of the strike the TAC(A) would make a low-level pass of his own for battle damage assessment (BDA), which was passed on to the withdrawing flight for their intelligence debriefing back at base.

The Marine battle report gave these examples of actual conversations during such an attack:

> TAC(A): Number One, from my smoke go six o'clock at 100 meters.

US Air Force forward air controllers work with a Korean radio operator to plan an air strike at a Republic of Korea 9 Division's landing zone. The USAF forward air controllers were assigned to the 21 Tactical Air Support Squadron. (Official US Air Force photo, Washington, DC)

       PILOT 1: Roger, One's in hot.
       TAC(A): I have you in sight, you're cleared to fire.
       PILOT 1: One's off target. Switches safe.
       TAC(A): Number Two, from One's hits come three o'clock at 50 meters.
       PILOT 2: Roger, Two's in hot.
       TAC(A): Your BDA follows: 5 KBA ["Killed by Air"]; two bunkers, 1 automatic weapon, and 50 meters trench line destroyed; one secondary explosion. You have been flying in support of the 26th Marines; your controller has been Southern Oscar. Good shooting and good afternoon, gentlemen.[4]

    Another innovation in close air support that started with Vietnam was ground-controlled radar bombing. These were described as being "as accurate and flexible as dive-bombing attacks and could be conducted in the worst weather. In fact, the technique was designed especially to cope with the inherent bad weather which accompanied the monsoons in Southeast Asia, when attack aircraft could not get below an overcast to hit the target."[5]
    Marine Air Support Squadron 3 moved its Air Support Radar Team Bravo (ASRT-B) into Khe Sanh on 16 January 1968. This team had

TPQ-10 radar linked to computers housed in a heavily reinforced van. The van, and the crew living quarters, was emplaced underground and heavily protected by sandbags. Thus the highly sensitive equipment remained operational all through the siege, even withstanding a direct hit by an enemy artillery shell on top of its bunker.

Inside the van the ground controllers operated their computers which were linked to the TPQ set, which itself sent out a slim pencil-shaped beam that detected and locked onto the aircraft. FSCC provided the target coordinates for the controllers to program in the Viet Cong positions, the wind speeds and directions, ballistic characteristics of the weapons being employed, and much other relevant data. The computer also automatically absorbed data input from the TPQ itself and returned to the aircraft airspeed and altitude corrections and gave correct headings to the observer to pass on to the pilot. The controller closely monitored each set and at the predetermined bomb-release point signaled a "Mark" to the pilot, who then released his bombs. (In pilot slang they "pickled" their ordnance). Usually TPQs (as such attacks became known) were made from 14,000 feet.

Special attack planes, like the A-4 Skyhawks and the A-6 Intruders, could even have their bombs released from the ground and not by the pilot! Each controller could handle single planes, sections (two aircraft), or divisions (four aircraft) on the same pass, provided the aircraft kept to a tight pattern and the radar did not break its lock. When the radar beam did stray from the aircraft, inputs to the computer were interrupted. The operator also lost visual contact on the radar screen.

The accuracy of TPQ attacks was described as "phenomenal." The flexibility of the system was demonstrated by the fact that a strike could be programmed and conducted within twelve minutes of request using any available airplane. In practice most of the TPQs were night strikes, when conventional dive-bombing was too dangerous. On 18 February 1968 for example, ASRT-B controlled aircraft that delivered 486 tons of ordnance on 105 separate targets in a twenty-four-hour period. During the whole siege, ASRT-B controlled 4,989 TPQs in support of the 26th Marines.

Each new air crew arriving at Khe Sanh conducted several trial missions before going "live." Normal first attempts resulted in forty-meter errors, but after the crew got used to the job there was an error rate of almost zero. Calibration drops were also carried out twice a week to ensure all the equipment was working correctly.

One member of the FSCC stated that, if he were in a foxhole and under attack, he would have no qualms about calling an ASRT-B controlled TPQ within 35 meters of his position. The rule of thumb that the

An air-to-air left side view of a US Marines' A-4M Skyhawk aircraft dropping two napalm canisters over a mountain area. The use of napalm in World War II was found effective in destroying dug-in infantrymen and it was extensively used thereafter in both Korea and Vietnam. (Official US Marine Corps photo, Washington, DC)

Jet delivery service. An A6-A Intruder of the US Marines' all-weather attack squadron No. 533 fulfills an order on 15 December 1967 for US Marine Division 7 on the ground in Vietnam. Members of this regiment, operating west of Da Nang, spotted a group of Viet Cong in the tree line and reported the enemy position to their forward air controller, who requested this radar-controlled bombing mission. (Official US Marine Corps photo, Washington, DC)

Inset
A dazzle-painted A-7 Corsair—the Short Ugly Little Fellah—one of the most cost-efficient ground support aircraft designed since World War II. (Official US air force photo)

Above
An A4-E Skyhawk attack jet drops its ordnance on a North Vietnamese position near Khe Sanh. One Marine Air Wing fighter and attack jets, plus artillery, accounted for 75 percent of the confirmed six hundred enemy killed during the action on Hill 881 South and North, two miles east of Khe Sanh during May 1967. (Official US Marine Corps photo, Washington, DC)

FSCC usually applied when determining a safe distance for normal operations, however, was one meter from the friendlies for every pound of conventional ordnance being delivered. Thus, for TPQs, a 250-pound bomb would not normally be dropped within 250 meters of allied troops, a 500-pounder within 500 meters, and so on. This criterion was not established because the men on the ground lacked confidence in the system but because of the large fragmentation pattern produced by the bombs.[6]

In the immediate aftermath of operation Niagara, which was the Communist army's greatest defeat ever by allied air power, the North Vietnamese High Command staked everything on the calculated sacrifice of the Viet Cong in a cyncial "publicity for bodies" all-out attack in the spring of 1968, the "Tet" offensive. This offensive was duly punished severely by the defenders with much help from fighter-bombers. Out of 84,000 Communist troops employed, 37,000 were killed and 6,000 wounded for an allied loss of 3,000 men. But the body count brought the North Vietnamese their reward in revulsion at the slaughter back in the United States. On 31 October 1968 the bombing was stopped and during the next three years the Americans pulled out.

While the "boys came home," the North Vietnamese used the lull to build up their conventional forces to an unparalleled degree. On 29 March 1971 they launched a massive invasion force of 150,000 regular troops across the DMZ spearheaded by 500 Soviet-built T-34, T-54, and PT-76 tanks, catching the south unprepared. Further attacks swung in through "neutral" Cambodia, the Central Highlands, and along the coast. The Americans had only seventy-six aircraft left in the country, F-4s and A-37s, and bad weather prevented even them from influencing events for some time.

More F-4s of the air force were rushed over, and several of the new UH-1B helicopters which had the new tube-launched optically-guided antitank weapon (TOW) on trial. This was a wire-guided missile. The marines added F-4s, A-4s, and the new EA-6A Intruders. These latter could carry an enormous punch, each Intruder taking into battle twenty-eight 500-pound bombs at a time. They soon proved their value and the toll of enemy tanks began to rise.

One of the best ground-support aircraft of this period was the Vought A-7A Corsair II, a subsonic jet nicknamed "SULF" (Short Ugly Little Fella). Certainly not much to look at, being a stubby, high-wing turbojet, the Corsair had a top speed of 533 knots at sea level which was pedestrian by modern standards. Nonetheless the Corsair was packed with lethal equipment that made it supreme in the close-support role.

The bomb load of the Corsair II was initially six low-drag Mk 82

500-pound general purpose (GP) bombs slung below the tubby little fuselage, with further capacity for up to 19,000 pounds of other rockets, missile, pods, or canisters on six underwing pylons. It had two fixed, single-barrel Colt-Browning Mk 12 20-mm cannon with 340 rounds per gun. Later models carried the 20-mm Vulcan M61 A1, rapid-fire cannon shooting tungsten-tipped shells, a deadly weapon against enemy armor. Continually developed modern versions can carry up to one hundred different types of ordnance in loads exceeding its own weight.

But it was not just its lifting capability or its economy that endeared the Corsair II to the three services. The weapons delivery system carried by the A-7A has been described as "probably one of the finest ever devised."[7] This system is built around an IBM digital computer linked to a precise internal guidance platform (PIPG). To get to the target area the pilot can punch in up to nine alternative destinations at a time. In return the computer estimates distance to target, time of flight, bearing, et cetera. This data is constantly updated and can be thrown onto a visual projected map display which shows the target and its immediate environs in graphic form. Once over the target the weapons can be delivered automatically by radar. The pilot can also use his Visual Attack mode in conjunction with a Head-Up Display (HUD) in front of his eyes and synchronize it with the aiming symbol on his cockpit canopy. The attacks were, of course, conducted in high-speed dives at any required angle. The results were very good, with accurate ordnance delivery on target. Against such sophistication the enemy ground troops stood little chance.

By midsummer, after much grievous fighting, tactical air power had halted the invasion. Using all the wide array of airborne weapons now available to them, high-explosive bombs, napalm, rockets, cluster bombs, laser- and television-guided bombs, and machine-gun fire, the Americans knocked out thousands of tanks, trucks, and vehicles. This enabled the South Vietnamese army to go on the offensive and retake vital towns and cities. The North Vietnamese were forced to return to the conference table in Paris, where they were to win by talk and deception what they had failed to take by armed might. The cease-fire was signed on 23 January 1973. In February 1975 the Communists returned in greater force than before and this time there was no help for the hapless South Vietnamese.

Air-support operations have been seen in many remote parts of the world in the last two decades. The most intensive operations were those over the Sinai desert in the various Israeli wars against their Arab neighbors. In the Six-Day War of 1967 Israel made a preemptive strike that knocked out the bulk of its potential enemies' air forces while they were

More specialized aircraft had to be developed to carry the increasing range of weapons for delivery against enemy ground targets as the 1960s passed into the 1970s and the sophistication of the ground-defense missile systems increased. Typical French answers were the D'Assault Mirage IIIC, IIIE, and Mirage 50 attack planes. These planes equipped the Israeli air force heavily in the Six Day War. (SHAA, Paris)

still on the ground. With complete air dominance, Israeli tanks swept forward across through the Sinai passes in the classic blitzkrieg manner, surrounding Egyptian armor and infantry, or merely bypassing them and leaving them to die in the waterless desert.

Equipped with eighteen French-built D'Assault Super Mystere B-2, fifty Mystere IV-A, seventy-two Mirage III-C, forty Duragan, and twenty-five Sud-Vautour IIA fighter-bombers, the Israeli air force was able to give total ground support to its three armored divisions in this lightning campaign. All these aircraft could carry large numbers of general-purpose bombs and 80-mm air-to-ground rockets in addition to their 30-mm DEFA cannon, 20-mm cannon, and 7.62-mm machine guns. The Vautours were the only specialized close-support machines, mounting four DEFA cannon along with two tons of mixed ordnance both internally and on underwing pylons. High on their training priorities had been practice ground-attack missions on the ranges in the Negev and they were also highly adept at fast turnaround rearming and refueling, which meant that a very high sortie rate could be maintained in combat.

The Egyptian commander, General Abdul Mortagy, had laid plans for an in-depth defense of his country with four infantry divisions stiffened with dug-in tanks and an armored group, Task Force Shazil, as a mobile counterblow force. The influence of their Soviet advisors was apparent—not only did the USSR supply the bulk of the armor, T34/85s and T54/55s, but also the tactics—a mini-Kursk was planned in the desert. For their ground-attack aircraft the Egyptians were mainly dependent on their older fighters of the Mikoyan MiG-15 and MiG-17 type backed up by forty Ilyushin Il-28 light, twin-jet bombers. Just coming in was a much more lethal aircraft, the Sukhoi Su-7B "Fitter-A" fighter-bomber, capable of Mach 1.6 speeds and armed with two Nr-30 cannon in the wing roots and 5,500 pounds of ordnance. But only one squadron of these was operational.

Under Operation "Red Sheet," dominance of the air over the battlefield enabled the Israeli attackers to keep on the move and maintain their momentum toward the Suez Canal at all times. The Egyptian 4 Armored Division moved up from Bir Gifgafa to smash the Israeli breakthrough at El Arish, but instead was ambushed and smashed by two waiting Israeli formations. The survivors were then caught by the fighter-bombers of the Israeli air force while streaming back to Jebel Libni and shattered by a deluge of bombs, napalm, and rockets.

Egyptian MiGs also carried out ground-attack sorties against the thrusting enemy armor, including one six-plane strike at columns approaching the Ismailia Pass on 7 June and thirty-two sorties the following day against reconnaissance spearheads heading for Suez. The scene was repeated in the days that followed at the Mitla Pass in the south.

However, by barring the pass with tanks, the Israelis forced the retreating Arabs into the desert where they were finished off by the strafing and bombing of the Mirages and Mysteres, backed by light bombers. By the end of the week 15,000 Arabs lay dead, 50,000 wounded, and 1,100 tanks had been lost at the cost of less than 700 Israeli dead. Of the forty-five aircraft lost, thirty-five went down to Arab return fire.

As a result of these battles the Arab States learned the lesson of the power of close air support and later rebuilt their armies with the specific intention of neutralizing that fateful effect on the battlefield. Heavy concentrations of Russian SA-2 "Guideline" missiles and the improved SA-3 (manned by Russian crews) surface-to-air missiles (SAMs) accompanied each ground unit and protected headquarters and other crucial areas. These had a medium-to-high capability up to 60,000 feet and a slant range of twenty-three miles. More important to the actual control over the battlefield's air space was the lavish use of the fully mobile SA-6 "Gainful" low-to-medium antiaircraft missile. This weapon mounted a radar-fire control unit incorporating the "Straight-Flush" continuous wave radar guidance system, which was unblockable by the Israeli countermeasures equipment. Each transporter-launcher vehicle carried three weapons. The SA-6 had a slant range of seventeen miles against low-flying aircraft. Also deployed were the SA-7 "Grail" infrared close-range missile, effective up to two miles, with a speed of Mach 1.5.

In the Vietnamese tradition the light antiaircraft weapons made a strong reappearance and large numbers of the ZSU-23-4, quadruple, 23-mm heavy automatic cannon, equipped with Gun Dish fire-control radar, were deployed. In this system control and direction were fully

A frightening degree of intensity and use of tactical air operations were the principal features of the various Israeli-Arab conflicts. Heavy losses were caused by the increasing use of surface-to-air missile defense systems to knock down low-flying jets. Here an Israeli Skyhawk napalms an Egyptian tank force during the Yom Kippur war. (Author's collection)

integrated and the weapon could fire fifty round bursts at a rate of fire of 4,000 rpm up to a height of 9,800 feet. In the air some eighty of the Su-7b ground-attack aircraft were also in service along with one hundred MiG-17 fighter-bombers.

When all was ready, the Egyptians recrossed the Suez Canal to liberate their eastern provinces on 6 October 1973, Yom Kippur, Israel's holiest day. All Egypt's two hundred fighter-bombers, Su-7Bs, MiG-21s, and -17s were thrown into attacks on Israeli defensive positions on the East Bank.

The expected Israeli counterblow was not long in coming, with their tank divisions now backed up with squadrons of American-supplied aircraft. These included 162 Douglas A-4H Skyhawks equipped with two 30-mm DEFA cannon and 127 MacDonnell F-4E Phantom fighter-bombers that could hoist six 750-pound GP bombs under the wings plus six 500-pound frag bombs under the fuselage. These attack planes also featured the latest Head-Up Display from Elliot Automation, the Lear Siegler inertial navigation system, and the Singer General Precision stabilized platform. This gave them vastly increased accuracy of ordnance delivery over the target.

Despite these high-tech upgrades, when they ran smack into the new Egyptian SAM systems, for the first time IAF squadrons began to take severe losses. By the third day they had lost fifty machines. The Egyptians claimed to have shot down sixteen Skyhawks in one day, 9 October. Despite this the Israelis continued to fly close-support missions of an almost suicidal nature, so desperate was their position on the ground in the Sinai.

The Egyptians won a sensational victory for the first time ever, but then their old caution reasserted itself. Instead of moving forward, their army halted to regroup. The SA-6s needed to be brought forward to be ready for the next blow. The Israelis took advantage of this lull to bring in their reserve armor and they, as always, did the job more quickly. Not until 14 October were the Egyptians ready, but then they found the situation changed in the air as well as on the ground.

The Americans had rushed in electronic countermeasure equipment, which included radar homing and warning receivers (RHAW); radar jamming pods and chaff to block the Egyptians' directional radar; "Walleye" glide bombs; Maverick television-sensor, air-to-ground anti-tank rockets; and Rockeye cluster bombs. The "Shrike" air-to-ground radiation-homing missile was used against the SAM sites by the Israeli air force and, on the ground, Israeli mobile columns gave these sites priority also.

The older Skyhawks were the most employed aircraft for close-support operations, and the Israeli air force lost fifty-two of their number in doing so. The Phantoms were mainly utilized in the interdiction and fighter-cover roles. It is interesting to note that the best method of destroying the troublesome SA-6 batteries was by attacks in high-angle dives—the old dive-bomber concept was proving as effective as ever.

When the Israelis counterattacked for a second time on 15 October they soon penetrated through to the Suez Canal and broke the Egyptian 2d Army at the so-called "Chinese Farm" position on the East Bank. They then crossed the canal itself to swing around to take the Egyptian 3d Army from the rear. It was all over soon after with the USSR and the United States forcing a cease-fire. The cost to the Israeli air force had been one hundred aircraft. But the very question of whether close-support aircraft could continue to operate in modern battle conditions was once again raised. In the continual seesaw between defender and attacker, the former looked once more to have the edge.

The frequent "little wars" that have abounded in the world since 1973 have proved to be less sophisticated in hardware or on a smaller scale than the Israeli/Arab conflicts. Even so, the role of the close air support aircraft has been shown to be indispensable in diverse situations. One was the Indo-Pakistan conflict over the Rann of Kutch. South African ground-attack aircraft, working out of Namibian forward airfields, gave valuable backing to Angolan insurgent forces. During the armed conflict between Great Britain and Argentina over the Falkland Islands, a second-rate naval power pitted a hodge-podge collection of overage (or unsuitable) antisubmarine warfare vessels against a third-rate air power.

The VTOL Harrier "Jump-jet" gave the media lots of copy, as did the effective use of the "Exocet" air-to-surface missile. Ground support was provided by RAF Harriers once the British got ashore, and the Argentines had a dozen of their IA.58 Pucara twin-engine attack planes on the islands, but it was small-scale stuff.

The front-line remains central Europe, and all manner of possible scenarios have been postulated in the last forty years as to what World War III might be like. Some theorize a "limited war" in which nuclear weapons will not be used and conventional forces will hammer it out to a stalemate. This is the optimistic view of course, but it is the only raison d'être for conventional weapons of all types.

The Soviets have introduced a whole series of "multirole" aircraft in the past decades. The Sukhoi Su-7B was developed progressively into the Su-20 "Fitter-C." The Sukhoi Su-19 "Fencer" appeared in the mid 1970s and was described as the first modern Soviet fighter to be developed specifically as a fighter-bomber for the ground-attack mission. A two-seat, variable-wing aircraft, it carries a single 23-mm GSh-23 twin-barreled cannon, which fires a 7-ounce projectile, and has six weapons pylons under the fuselage. This has been steadily improved to the Su-24 "Fencer" attack aircraft.

Meanwhile the MiG series continued through the superlative MiG-19 "Farmer" which could carry various FAB (free-falling aerial bomb) bombs of up to 1,100 pounds, cluster-bomb canisters containing PTK bomblets, UV-16-57 and UV-32-57 multiple launchers for firing the standard Soviet 57-mm ground-attack rocket, and the powerful S-24 240-mm rocket on single pylons. It was also equipped with BETAB retarded rocket-boosted penetrators for use against concrete installations. It has been widely exported.

The series has moved on to include the MiG-23 "Flogger" interceptor, which is a single-seater powered by a Tumansky R-29B Turbojet and armed with a 23-mm GSg-23 cannon as well as weapons pods, and the much larger MiG-25 "Foxbat." Rocketing of Afghan rebel forces featured extensively in that long war in the classic "colonial" model, but again hand-held "Blowpipe" missiles caused a more cautious deployment of these sophisticated aircraft against the Mujad Hadeen insurgents.

The ultimate NATO tank-buster is the Fairchild Republic A-10 Thunderbolt II attack aircraft. The USAF initiated this project in the 1970s when the old A-1 Skyraider was being pensioned off and they considered the need for a machine capable of dealing with the antiair threat posed by various surface-to-air missiles and the quad 23-mm heavy machine guns. A higher transit speed to the target was called for and a

A Soviet MiG-21 conducts a low-level pass during Warsaw Pact exercises in the early 1980s. (Author's collection)

An American air force Fairchild Republic A-10A Thunderbolt II aircraft of the United States Air Force Europe's tactical wing, based in Great Britain. The aircraft was mainly built around the enormously powerful General Electric GAU-8/A Avenger seven-barreled 30-mm gatling-type rotary cannon. This gun, some twenty-two feet long, is the most awesome conventional aerial antitank weapon yet devised. (Author's collection, courtesy of USAFE)

An aerial view of the A-10 Thunderbolt II aircraft showing the twin tail layout, the massive engines located abaft the wings, the payload of weaponry below the wings, and the nose of the massive tank crunching cannon. (Official US Air Force photo)

turboprop engine system was originally planned. However, the increased loading requirements brought about a switch to the new, and more reliable, turbofan. The design requirements for the aircraft resulted in a very distinctive machine, the AX-1.

Although not designed from the outset as such, the AX-1 was soon seen as primarily a tank-stopper. Its role was to try to offset the four-to-one numerical superiority in tanks and armored vehicles the Warsaw Pact holds over the West. Accordingly the massive GAU-8A 30-mm cannon was adopted for this purpose.

The Thunderbolt is a single-seat, midwing, twin-boom aircraft, designed to operate at low level. It is not a pretty machine (its nickname is the "Warthog") any more than the German Stuka was, but like the

Stuka, it is highly efficient at the task for which it is built. Flying low and level and using low-drag bombs, it proved highly accurate in trials. It proved itself much more maneuverable than the A-7 Corsair II, for example, and was capable of absorbing much more punishment. Due to its very efficient, low-speed wing configuration and low fuel consumption, the A-10 had that other vital ingredient, the ability to linger over the target zone.

It is powered by two General Electric TF34-GE-100 turbofan jet engines, which are rated at 9,065 pounds thrust each, and has a top speed of 385 knots at sea level in level flight. It has a designed diving speed of 450 knots. The engines are set well back off the rear fuselage and it has twin booms for stability. This leaves the pilot positioned well forward with excellent vision, and the fuselage and wings are left unclut-tered for eleven weapons pylons for mounting various ordnance loads.

At its maximum weight the A-10 can carry eighteen Mk-82 500-pound bombs, 1,350 rounds of 30-mm ammunition, and 10,650 pounds of internal fuel. Its systems include the Pave Penny laser ranger and target seeker and inertial navigation. Consideration is being given to upgrading further by fitting the low-altitude navigation targeting infra-red night system (LANTIRN) to increase its flexibility.

Even the ability of this awesome machine to hold the Warsaw Pact tank breakthroughs is being questioned, while the role of the helicopter in immediate close air support is being touted more and more. The cur-rent AH-64 is claimed to be the best antitank and quick reaction close air support weapon in the West. But its vulnerability to hand-held anti-aircraft weapons like the Blowpipe, as well as opposing helicopter gun-ships, is obvious. The value of the A-10's ability to linger is in question because current thought suggests that the battlefield of a future Euro-pean war will be no place for aircraft to hang around in. A repeat of the Fairey Battle massacres seems in the cards if lingering is tried with the weight, power, and sophistication of antiaircraft weaponry available to the Soviets. With the Eastern bloc having some 25,000 tanks at instant readiness against a NATO mishmash of 7,000, just how many T72s will the A-10s have to knock out to even things up? An impossible task, even supposing they can stay alive long enough to conduct multiple missions.

Since June 1985 the talk has been of cheaper alternatives to provide more "one-pass" machines to do the job more successfully, more often, and live to tell the tale. The air force issued a request for ideas to fill the proposed close air support-X (CAS-X) concept to complement the A-10. Northrop came up with their F-20A, General Dynamics the F-16C, and McDonnell Douglas the AV-8B. Chief contender for the close air support role is the Vought A-7X Strikefighter, yet another revision of the long-standing A-7 Corsair II. The proposition is to rebuild existing A-7s, with a stretch to the fuselage, LERX "strakes" to improve lift, an afterburning turbofan engine, and increased and enhanced sensor provision.

Whatever the decision, and that depends, as usual, on funding, any new close air support aircraft would probably have to incorporate most if not all of the following state-of-the-art technology, in both target-finding and electronic countermeasures (ECM) roles, to be efficient.

1. Holographic, wide-angle HUD, with three multifunction displays (two color, one monochrome), with hands-on throttle and stick (HOTAS) operation.

2. Night-vision-goggle-compatible CHEAP NIGHT system.

3. Hypervelocity missile system.

4. Tricor ALE-40 chaff/IR dispenser to block enemy radar.

5. Air-intercept missiles, like the AIM-9L/M Sidewinder infrared antiaircraft missile (AAM) stations.

6. Martin Marietta LANTIRN night-attack sensor pods with FLIR (forward-looking infrared) laser designator/ranger, automatic target recognition and tracking pod with IR sensors, scanners and pointing equipment with video recorder provision. Either wide or narrow field display, controlled through the navigation/weapons delivery system, NWDS, incorporating Maverick, Ku band terrain avoidance radar (TAR).

7. APQ-26 radar.

A Royal Air Force SEPECAT Jaguar GR. Mk.1 ground-attack aircraft, equipped with the RAF's version of Texas Instrument's Paveway laser-guided bombs for "stand-off" attacks against enemy armor and troop concentrations. (Author's collection, courtesy of Texas Instruments, Inc.)

8. Ring-laser gyro, permitting takeoff roll within two minutes of cold start with minimum drift.

9. Capacity to work with global positioning system (GPS) of satellite-based autonomous navigation system. This enables an aircraft to know its precise location to within sixteen meters in three dimensions.

10. PAVE/PENNY laser target location.

11. ALQ-165/184 ASPJs (advance self-protection jammer system).

12. ALR-74 radar warning receiver.

13. ARC 164 (UHF) and ARC 186 (VHF) radios.

14. Single-channel ground-to-air radio system (SINCGARS).

15. Increased cooling capacity to compensate for all the equipment above.

All this gadgetry is now considered essential to delivery of the following ordnance: "Dumb" bombs, precision-guided munitions (PGMs), CBU2A and CBU-52 cluster bombs, and M-61 Vulcan cannon firing 3.5-ounce armor-piercing and high-explosive incendiary projectiles.

Application of this hardware and software would result in a multimillion-dollar aircraft, no matter how it is done, and this very expensive piece of flying hardware might well be sent out against a Soviet T-72 tank. This concept of "a sledgehammer to crack a nut" is making close air support look increasingly unviable in the years ahead.[8]

Even more of a threat to the close air support concept is the further development of hand-held missiles. Once again design work was initiated by the Swedes, who have always been in the forefront of weapons technology, be it the Bofors gun, the Wilkensen dive-bomber sight, or the Draaken interceptor. The Swedes have again come up with a weapon that has shaken the thinking of the major air powers to its very foundations. This is the RBS 70, "man-portable" surface-to-air missile, which is a laser-beam rider. Not one of the existing detection or warning sensors carried by aircraft can block this weapon. It makes the highly vul-

The ultimate troop-killing machine. The modern refined ground-attack fighter-bomber, like this F-20 Tigershark, packs a lethal dose of military hardware that can be delivered with deadly precision into the enemy's lap. The great disparity in numbers between the armies of the West and the Communist forces in Europe makes the delivery of such ordnance from the air absolutely essential for NATO to hold the line. (Author's collection, courtesy of Gerald Balzer)

A US Air Force General Dynamic F-16C fighter-bomber releases a Paveway I GBU-10 laser-guided "smart bomb." With such sophisticated weaponry the modern close-support aircraft can "stand off" from its target and deliver its punch with relative immunity from hand-held antiaircraft missile systems. (Author's collection, courtesy of Texas Instruments, Inc.)

nerable forward air control redundant and gives the ground troops an awesome accuracy, no matter what the weather conditions.

But whatever the future, if wars there be, then to the Poor Bloody Infantryman (PBI being the original and ultimate acronym of War—past and present), the sight of a friendly aircraft accurately delivering massive doses of explosive into the enemy ahead will always be a welcome, if increasingly scarce, sight in any armed conflict.

Source Notes

2: FORGING AND APPLYING THE WEAPON

1. Headquarters of Royal Flying Corps, unpublished memorandum to Major Maurice Musgrave, October 1914 (Public Record Office, London, file Air.1).
2. Captain Geoffrey Dugdale in Bryan Cooper, *The Ironclads of Cambrai*, Pan Books, London, 1970, pp. 175–76.
3. Colonel T. E. Lawrence, *Revolt in the Desert*, George Doran, New York, 1927, p. 289.
4. General Sir Edmund Ironside, Chief of the British Imperial General Staff. See Colonel R. Macleod, *The Ironside Diaries, 1939–40*, Cassell, London, 1956.
5. Major James P. Yancey, official report, 24 August 1919 (National Archives and Records Service, Washington, DC). See also Stacey C. Hinkle, *Wings and Saddles*: *The Air and Cavalry Punitive Expedition of 1919*, volume V, number 3, University of Texas at El Paso, Texas, 1967, p. 35.
6. Admiral F. D. Wagner, US Navy, unpublished interview with Major General Ross Erastus Rowell, US Marine Corps 24 October 1946 (US Marine Corps Aviation History Unit Archive, Washington, DC).

3: THEORIES AND PRACTICE

1. Lieutenant David B. Overfield, US Navy, "Dive Bombing Compared with Level Flight," unpublished lecture, US Navy War College, 1939, pp. 9–16 (US Navy Archives, Washington, DC). Also, Commander B. G. Leighton, US Navy, "The Relation between Air and Surface Activities in

the Navy," unpublished lecture, US Navy War College, 1928 (US Navy Archives, Washington, DC). Also, Captain Vernon E. McGee, US Marine Corps, "Dive Bombing," unpublished lecture, 1937 (US Marine Corps Archives, Washington, DC). Copies in author's collection.

2. Colonel Nils Kindberg, Royal Swedish Air Force (*Flygvapnet*), Stockholm, "Outline of the History of Dive Bombing in Sweden," unpublished memorandum compiled for the author, 1978. See also Anonymous, "Svenskt Flyg ock dess Man," *KSAK* magazine, Stockholm, Sweden, 1976.

3. Eberhard Spetzler, *Luftkreig und Menschlichkeit*, Musterschmidt, Gottingen, 1956, pp. 36–37. See also Hanfried Schliephake, *The Birth of the Luftwaffe*, Ian Allan, Shepperton, UK, 1971, p. 39.

4. Luftwaffe General Staff, "Tactical Requirements Summary," Berlin, March 1938 (*Militargeschichtliches Forschungsamt* Archives, Freiburg, West Germany).

5. Sir Maurice Dean, *The R.A.F.: A History*, Cassel, London, 1985.

6. British Air Ministry, "Meeting to Consider Dive Bombing," unpublished memorandum, 19 September 1938 (Public Record Office, London, file Air2/1787/04881).

7. Sir Maurice Dean, *The R.A.F.: A History*, Cassel, London, 1985.

8. British Air Ministry, "Dive Bombing," unpublished memorandum, London, 1939.

9. British Air Ministry, "Air Intelligence Report, Number 31: Japanese Air to Ground Tactics in China," unpublished memorandum, London, 1936 (Public Record Office, London, file Air5/1137/04811).

10. Hugh Thomas, *The Spanish Civil War*, Penguin, London, 1977, pp. 237–38.

11. Air Vice Marshal J. R. Walker, CBE, AFC, RAF, *Air-to-Ground Operations*, volume 2, Brassey's Defence Publishers, London, 1987, pp. 100–101.

12. British Air Ministry, *The Rise and Fall of the Luftwaffe*, A.C.A.S. (I) His Majesty's Stationery Office, London, 1948.

13. Luftwaffe Lieutenant Hans Asmus in Gordon Thomas and Max Morgan-Watts, *The Day Guernica Died*, London, 1975, p. 212.

4: SCHWERPUNKT!

1. Luftwaffe General Staff, "Tactical Requirements Summary," Berlin, March 1938 (*Militargeschichtliches Forschungsamt* archives, Freiburg, West Germany).

2. *The Rise and Fall of the Luftwaffe*. pp. 42–43.

3. *Ibid*, p. 54.

4. General A. Armengaud, *Batailles politiques et militaires sur l'Europe*, Paris, 1948.

5. *The Rise and Fall of the Luftwaffe*, p. 57.

6.   General Kutrzeba, Polish Field Commander, September 1939, in Cajus Bekker, *The Luftwaffe War Diaries*, Corgi Books, London, 1969, p. 74.

7.   Sergeant-Gunner Conill in Robert Jackson, *Air War over France*, Ian Allan, Shepperton, 1974, p. 61.

8.   Bryan Perrett, *A History of Blitzkrieg*, Robert Hale, London, 1983, p. 92.

9.   *The Rise and Fall of the Luftwaffe*, p. 70.

10.   British Air Ministry, "Dive Bombing: A Review of Policy," unpublished memorandum, 9 May 1940 (Public Record Office, London, file Air2/3176/S4583).

11.   British Air Ministry, "Summary of Air Intelligence Report, Number 302," unpublished memorandum, May 1940 (Public Record Office, London, file Air2/22/9/04811).

12.   Lieutenant General Helmut Mahlke, unpublished letters to the author, 1976–77.

13.   British Air Ministry, unpublished memorandum to Minister of Aircraft Production, 9 December 1940 (Public Record Office, London, file Air14/181/IIH/241/3/406).

14.   *Ibid.*

15.   Air Vice Marshal J. C. Slessor, Royal Air Force, "Use of Bombers in Close Support of the Army," unpublished memorandum, 6 May 1941 (Public Record Office, London, file Air20/2970).

16.   Compton Mackenzie, *Wind of Freedom*, Chatto and Windus, London, 1943, pp. 175–76. See also Ministry of Information, "The Campaign in Greece and Crete," His Majesty's Stationery Office, London, 1943.

5: ATTRITION AND ADJUSTMENT

1.   Colonel N. Desnisov, *Boyevaia Slava Sovetskai Aviatsii*, Voenizdat, Moscow, 1962, pp. 92–97.

2.   M. N. Kozhevnikov, *The Command and Staff of the Soviet Army Air Force in the Great Patriotic War 1941–1945: A Soviet View*, US Air Force translation, US Government Printing Office, Washington, DC, 1982, pp. 84–85.

3.   *Ibid.*

4.   Army Air Force, "Summary of the A-35 Airplane Project," unpublished memorandum, USAAF document number 202-1-3, September 1943 (Department of Air Force History, Washington, DC).

5.   *Ibid.*

6.   Walter D. Edmonds, *They Fought with What They Had*, Little, Brown, Boston, 1951, p. 208.

7.   *Ibid.*, pp. 229–230.

8.   Air Chief Marshal Sir Robert Brooke-Popham, interview, *Sydney Herald*, September 1941, in Walter D. Edmonds, *They Fought with*

What They Had, Little, Brown, Boston, 1951, p. 254. See also Lieutenant General A. E. Percival, *The War in Malaya*, Eyre and Spottiswoode, London, 1949. See also Russell Grenfell, *Main Fleet to Singapore*, Faber and Faber, London, 1951, pp. 75–77, 81–91.

9.   British Air Ministry, Vice Chief of the Air Staff, unpublished memorandum, to Secretary of State for Air, 16 March 1942 (Public Record Office, London, file Air2/5504).

10.   *Ibid.*

11.   Document prepared by Sir Stafford Cripps 2 July 1942, for Prime Minister, paragraph 6. Winston S. Churchill, *The Second World War*, volume 4, *The Hinge of Fate*, Cassell, London, 1951, pp. 354–55. Winston S. Churchill, unpublished Prime Minister's personal minute to the Chief of the Air Staff, 14 July 1941 (Public Record Office, London, file Air8/631).

12.   Basil H. Liddell Hart, *History of the Second World War*, Cassell, London, 1970, p. 99. See also Winston S. Churchill, *The Second World War*, volume 2, *The Hinge of Fate*, Cassell, London, 1951, pp. 592–93.

13.   Daniel R. Mortensen, *A Pattern for Joint Operations: World War II Close Air Support North Africa*, Office of Air Force History and US Army Center of Military History, Washington, DC, 1987, pp. 59–61.

6: EXPANSION AND LIMITATIONS

1.   John B. Watson, unpublished letters to the author, 1986–87.

2.   Admiral Francis Laine, French navy, unpublished letters to the author, 1986–87.

3.   *Ibid.*

4.   French navy official, unpublished combat reports of 3d Air Flotilla, French navy, April–May 1944. Copies supplied to author by Admiral Laine.

5.   Admiral Francis Laine, French navy, unpublished letters to the author, April–May 1987.

6.   French navy official, unpublished combat reports of 3d Air Flotilla, French navy, April–May 1944. Copies supplied to author by Admiral Laine.

7.   Lieutenant Robert P. Friesz, US Navy, in Robert Olds, *Helldiver Squadron*, Dodd, Mead and Co., New York, 1946, pp. 140–41.

8.   Lieutenant Commander Geoffrey P. Norman, US Navy, in Robert Olds, *Helldiver Squadron*, Dodd, Mead and Co., New York, 1946, p. 141.

9.   Lieutenant Colonel William H. Jones, APO, India, unpublished letter to Morris Tombler, Nashville, Tenn., 8 November 1942 (Consolidated Vultee Aircraft Incorporation file copy, ref. 142 16–23, pp. 1–2). Copy in author's files.

10.   British Air Ministry and the Central Office of Information, Lon-

don, *Wings of the Phoenix*, His Majesty's Stationery Office, London, 1949, p. 126.

11.   *Ibid.*, p. 127.

12.   Wing Commander Arthur M. Gill, Royal Air Force, interviews with and letters to the author, 1985–87.

13.   *Ibid.*

14.   *Ibid.*

15.   Soviet Official History, *The Soviet Air Force in World War II*, translated into English by Leland Fetzer, David and Charles, Newton Abbot, UK, 1974, p. 372.

16.   *Ibid.*, p. 373.

17.   *Ibid.*, p. 373.

18.   *Ibid.*, p. 375.

7: REDUCTION AND REVIVAL

1.   Bernard B. Fall, *Hell in a Very Small Place: The Siege of Dien Bien Phu*, Da Capo, New York, 1985, pp. 44–45.

2.   *Ibid.*, p. 101.

3.   Jules Roy, *The Battle of Dienbienphu*, Carroll and Graf Publishers, Inc., New York, 1984, pp. 71–75.

4.   Captain A. Patou, *Rapport d'operations; forces maritimes; groupe porte avions d'extreme orient, 26 Decembre 1953 au 2 Juin 1954*, unpublished. Copies presented to the author by Captain Patou. Also, unpublished correspondence and memoirs from M. H. de Lestapis to the author, 1986. See also General L. M. Chassin, *Aviation Indochine*, Amiot Dumont, Paris, 1954, pp. 205–16.

5.   Bernard B. Fall, pp. 203–204.

6.   *Ibid.*, p. 210.

7.   Anonymous, "The Air-Ground Operation in Korea," *Air Force* magazine, Washington, DC, March 1951, volume 34, number 3, pp. 19–58.

8.   Major Michael J. Dolan, "What's Right and Wrong with Close Air Support," *Combat Forces Journal*, Washington, DC, July 1951, volume 1, number 12, p. 24.

9.   *Ibid.*, pp. 24–25.

10.   General Mark W. Clark, "What Kind of Air Support Does the Army Want?" interview in *Air Force* magazine, Washington, DC, December 1950, volume 33, number 12, pp. 24–25, 52.

11.   *Ibid.*

12.   *Ibid.*

13.   Dolan, pp. 25 *et seq.*

14.   General Hoyt S. Vandenberg, US Air Force Chief of Staff, "The Air-Ground Operation in Korea: If You See a Pilot . . . ," *Air Force* magazine, Washington, DC, March 1951, volume 34, number 3, p. 43.

15.   *Ibid.*

16. Anonymous, "Out of Millions of Words . . . , Confusion, Doubt and Concern," *Air Force* magazine, Washington, DC, March 1951, volume 34, number 3, p. 18.
17. *Ibid.*
18. *Ibid.*
19. *Ibid.*
20. General J. Lawton Collins, US Army Chief of Staff, "The Air-Ground Operations in Korea," *Air Force* magazine, Washington, DC, March 1951, volume 34, number 3, p. 39.

8: NEW LESSONS AND MICROCHIP TECHNOLOGY

1. US Marine Corps, *The Battle for Khe Sanh*, official account, History and Museums Division Headquarters, US Marine Corps, Washington, DC, 1975, p. 93. See also US Marine Corps, *First Marine Air Wing's Command Chronology and Narrative Accounts*, January and February, 1968, unpublished, declassified combat reports. Copies in author's archives.
2. *Ibid.*, p. 94.
3. *Ibid.*, pp. 94–95.
4. *Ibid.*, p. 97.
5. *Ibid.*, p. 103.
6. *Ibid.*, p. 104.
7. Anonymous, *World's Greatest Attack Aircraft*, Oriole Publishing, London, 1988.
8. Air Vice Marshal J. R. Walker, CBE, AFC, RAF, *Air-to-Ground Operations*, volume 2, Brassey's Defence Publishers, London, 1987, pp. 123–26.

Sources

Anonymous. "The Air-Ground Operation in Korea." *Air Force*. March 1951, vol. 34, no. 3.

Anonymous. "Out of Millions of Words . . . Confusion, Doubt and Concern." *Air Force*. March 1951, vol. 34, no. 3.

Anonymous. *The Soviet Air Force in World War II*. Translated by Leland Fetzer. (Newton Abbot, UK: David and Charles, 1974).

Anonymous. "Svenskt Flyg och dess Man," *KSAK*. Stockholm, 1976.

Anonymous. *World's Greatest Attack Aircraft*. (London: Oriole Publishing, 1988).

Armengaud, A., General. *Batailles politiques et militaires sur l'Europe*. (Paris: 1948).

Bekker, Cajus. *The Luftwaffe War Diaries*. (London: Corgi Books, 1969).

British Air Ministry, "Air Intelligence Report Number 31: Japanese Air to Ground Tactics in China," unpublished memorandum, 1936. Public Record Office, London, file Air5/1137/04811.

———."Dive Bombing," unpublished memorandum, 1939.

———."Dive Bombing: A Review of Policy," unpublished memorandum, 9 May 1940. Public Record Office, London, file Air2/3176/S4583/.

———."Meeting to Consider Dive Bombing," unpublished memorandum, 19 September 1938. Public Record Office, London, file Air2/1787/04881/.

————.*The Rise and Fall of the Luftwaffe, A.C.A.S. (I).* (London: His Majesty's Stationery Office, 1948).

————."Summary of Air Intelligence Report, Number 302," unpublished memorandum, May 1940. Public Record Office, London, file Air2/22/9/04811.

————.Unpublished memorandum to Minister of Aircraft Production, 9 December 1940. Public Record Office, London, file Air14/181/IIH/241/3/406.

————.Unpublished memorandum to Secretary of State for Air, 16 March 1942. Public Record Office, London, file Air2/5504.

British Air Ministry and the Central Office of Information. *Wings of the Phoenix.* (London: His Majesty's Stationery Office, 1949).

Chassin, L. M., General. *Aviation Indochine.* (Paris: Amiot Dumont, 1954).

Churchill, Winston S. *The Second World War: Volume IV, The Hinge of Fate.* (London: Cassell, 1951).

————.Unpublished personal minutes to the Chief of the Air Staff, 14 July 1941. Public Record Office, London, file Air8/631.

Clark, Mark W., General. "What Kind of Air Support Does the Army Want?" Interview in *Air Force.* December 1950, vol. 33, no. 12.

Collins, J. Lawton, General, and General Hoyt S. Vandenberg. "The Air-Ground Operations in Korea." *Air Force.* March 1951, vol. 34, no. 3.

Cooper, Bryan. *The Ironclads of Cambrai.* (London: Pan Books, 1970).

Dean, Maurice, Sir. *The R.A.F.: A History.* (London: Cassell, 1985).

de Lestapis, M. H. Unpublished correspondence and memoirs, 1986.

Desnisov, N., Colonel. *Boyevaia Slava Sovetskai Aviatsii.* (Moscow: Voenizdat, 1962).

Dolan, Michael J., Major. "What's Right and Wrong with Close Air Support." *Combat Forces Journal.* July 1951, vol. 1, no. 12.

Edmonds, Walter D. *They Fought with What They Had.* (Boston: Little, Brown, 1951).

Fall, Bernard B. *Hell in a Very Small Place: The Siege of Dien Bien Phu.* (New York: Da Capo, 1985).

French navy. Unpublished combat reports of 3d Air Flotilla, April–May 1944.

Gill, Arthur M., Wing Commander. Interviews with and letters to the author, 1985–87.

Grenfell, Russell. *Main Fleet to Singapore.* (London: Faber and Faber, 1951).

Hart, Basil H. Liddell. *History of the Second World War.* (London: Cassell, 1970).

Hinkle, Stacey C. *Wings and Saddles: The Air and Cavalry Punitive*

Expedition of 1919, vol. 5, no. 3. (El Paso, Texas: University of Texas, 1967).

Jackson, Robert. *Air War over France*. (Shepperton, UK: Ian Allan, 1974).

Jones, William H., Lieutenant Colonel. Unpublished letter to Morris Tombler, 8 November 1942. (Consolidated Vultee Aircraft file copy ref. 142 16–23).

Kindberg, Nils, Colonel. "Outline of the History of Dive Bombing in Sweden," unpublished memorandum.

Kozhevnikov, M. N. *The Command and Staff of the Soviet Army Air Force in the Great Patriotic War 1941–1945: A Soviet View*. Washington: US Government Printing Office, 1982.

Laine, Francis, Admiral. Unpublished letters to the author, 1986–87.

Lawrence, T. E., Colonel. *Revolt in the Desert*. (New York: George Doran, 1927).

Leighton, B. G., Commander. "The Relation Between Air and Surface Activities in the Navy," unpublished lecture, US Navy War College, 1928. US Navy Archives, Washington, DC.

Luftwaffe General Staff. "Tactical Requirements Summary." Berlin: March 1938. *Militargeschichtliches Forschungsamt* Archives, Freiburg, West Germany.

Mackenzie, Compton. *Wind of Freedom*. (London: Chatto and Windus, 1943).

Macleod, R., Colonel. *The Ironside Diaries, 1939–40*. (London: Cassell, 1956).

Mahlke, Helmut, Lieutenant General. Unpublished letters to the author, 1976–77.

McGee, Vernon E., Captain. "Dive Bombing," unpublished lecture, 1937. US Marine Corps Archives, Washington, DC.

Ministry of Information. "The Campaign in Greece and Crete." (London: His Majesty's Stationery Office, 1943).

Mortensen, Daniel R. *A Pattern for Joint Operations: World War II Close Air Support North Africa*. (Washington, DC: Office of Air Force History and US Army Center of Military History, 1987).

Olds, Robert. *Helldiver Squadron*. (New York: Dodd, Mead and Co., 1946).

Overfield, David B., Lieutenant. "Dive Bombing Compared with Level Flight," unpublished lecture, US Navy War College, 1939. US Navy Archives, Washington, DC.

Patou, A., Captain. *Rapport d'operations; forces maritimes; groupe porte avions d'extreme orient, 26 Decembre 1953 au 2 Juin 1954*, unpublished.

Percival, A. E., Lieutenant General. *The War in Malaya*. (London: Eyre and Spottiswoode, 1949).

Perrett, Bryan. *A History of Blitzkrieg*. (London: Robert Hale, 1983).

Roy, Jules. *The Battle of Dienbienphu*. (New York: Carroll and Graf Publishers, Inc., 1984).

Royal Flying Corps, Headquarters of. Unpublished memorandum to Major Maurice Musgrave, October 1914. Public Record Office, London, file Air.1.

Schliephake, Hanfried. *The Birth of the Luftwaffe*. (Shepperton, UK: Ian Allan, 1971).

Slessor, J. C., Air Vice Marshal. "Use of Bombers in Close Support of the Army," unpublished memorandum, 6 May 1941. Public Record Office, London, file Air 20/2970.

Spetzler, Eberhard. *Luftkreig und Menschlichkeit*. (Gottingen, West Germany: Musterschmidt, 1956).

Stewart, Adrian. *The Underrated Enemy: Britain's War with Japan*. (London: William Kimber, 1987).

Thomas, Gordon, and Max Morgan-Watts. *The Day Guernica Died*. (London: 1975).

Thomas, Hugh. *The Spanish Civil War*. (London: Penguin, 1977).

US Army Air Force. "Summary of the A-35 Airplane Project," unpublished memorandum, USAAF document number 202-1-3, September 1943. Department of Air Force History, Washington, DC.

US Marine Corps. *The Battle for Khe Sanh*. History and Museums Division Headquarters, US Marine Corps, Washington, DC.

———.*First Marine Air Wing's Command Chronology and Narrative Accounts*, January and February 1968, unpublished.

Wagner, F. D., Admiral. Unpublished interview with Major General Ross Erastus Rowell, 24 October 1946. Marine Corps Aviation History Unit Archive, Washington, DC.

Walker, J. R., Air Vice Marshal. *Air-to-Ground Operations*, vol. 2. (London: Brassey's Defence Publishers, 1987).

Watson, John B. Unpublished letters to the author, 1986–87.

Yancy, James P., Major. Official report, 24 August 1919. National Archives and Records Service, Washington, DC.

Index

Index